The Invisible Struggle

Donna and Mike,
God bless!
Faye

The Invisible Struggle

Faye Farnsworth

Library of Congress Control Number: 2009913523

ISBN:	Hardcover	978-1-4500-1403-8
	Softcover	978-1-4500-1402-1
	Ebook	978-1-4500-1404-5

This book was printed in the United States of America.

To order additional copies of this book, contact:
Xlibris Corporation
1-888-795-4274
www.Xlibris.com
Orders@Xlibris.com
72155

CONTENTS

Dedication

I dedicate this book to my children and grandchildren. I hope they find some of their stories hidden within these pages. They are my inspiration.

I also want to acknowledge the support and time that my dear husband, Keith, has given during the writing process—a process which included being ignored, barked at, and then asked to contribute ideas and time to evaluate and read. Thanks also to friends Beulah and Mark and to two granddaughters who read the manuscript, proofed, and gave suggestions.

Without their help, this book would not have happened.

The Author

Glossary/Credit of Coined Words/Names Used in *The Invisible Struggle*

Good One:	A name used for God, the rightful ruler of the universe.
Guerdon:	A name used for Jesus, who is a member of God's family and came to earth on the rescue mission for humans. The name means "reward," "recompense."
Zephyr:	A member of God's family who is sometimes called God's Spirit, the Holy Spirit, the Comforter, or the Advocate. The name Zephyr means a soft, gentle breeze.
Fifth dimension:	A term used in the book as the space that the heavenly beings operate in. It is usually invisible to human beings, but with the aid of the special green glasses, our human heroes are able to see this dimension.
Golden angels:	Invisible heavenly beings who help God's family take care of human beings on earth. They are sometimes called guardian angels.
Evil angels:	Invisible heavenly beings who rebelled against God and his kingdom long ago. They and their leader, Hesperus, work against all in God's kingdom, including human beings.

Kanana: A name of endearment that the heavenly beings applied to human beings. Its origin is from the Shona language and means "small child."

Hesperus: The heavenly angel who rebelled against God and is the cause for evil in the universe. He is also known as the devil, Satan, or Lucifer. (Lucifer and Hesperus are ancient names for the planet Venus.)

R-dor: The capital of God's kingdom located in outer space. It is sometimes called heaven and is based on love.

Credit note: The New International Version of the Bible is used when scripture is quoted.

Prologue

Eons and eons ago the universe came into being at the breath of the Good One. The capital of the universe was named R-dor (pronounced Arr-door) and was placed on the planet of Orb. The inhabitants of the kingdom lived, played, and worked in perfect harmony. The Good One and his family were the rulers and servants of all. The living creatures, the angels, and the beasts helped the king and one another. They built, beautified, gardened, and grew with one another. The air was filled with light, music, and laughter.

Then one day the mystery began. The shining angel, Hesperus, became very enchanted with his reflection in the Lake of Life. Every day, he flew to the lake to admire his reflection. Every day, he became more and more in love with his reflection. And every day, he became less and less in love with the king and everyone else. Eventually, Hesperus thought he was more beautiful than anyone, even the king. Hesperus started whispering to himself, "You are very beautiful! You are very beautiful!"

The wise king, who hears and knows everything, decided to talk to Hesperus. "Beautiful star, I hear you whispering to yourself. Why are you so much in love with yourself? You know the way to happiness is to love everyone else as much as you love yourself. See how you are becoming stooped over. You are spending too much time looking at your reflection in the lake. Soon, you will not be able to stand up straight. You are losing your balance. You should stay away from the lake until you can stand up straight again."

Hesperus did not want to stay away from the lake, so he went anyway. He wanted to see his reflection every day. He began to whisper out, very quietly at first, then louder and louder. Other angels heard the whispers, and they started whispering, too. One day, the king, who had heard the whispers from the very beginning, decided it was time to talk to the angels. "Why are you whispering?

Do you not know that it is safe to speak out loud? Are you ashamed of what you are speaking? Please speak the truth."

Hesperus did not want to speak the truth. His whispers had become lies. His words became threats. His heart changed from softness to hardness. His respect for others turned into jealousy. He wanted to have his own way all the time. He rebelled against the king and the ways of the kingdom. He wanted to start his own kingdom.

The king said, "This is not good. The harmony is gone. The music is gone. The laughter is gone. Hesperus and his followers must leave."

"We won't leave," insisted Hesperus. "Let me be the king, and I will make things good again."

"You can't," replied Good One. "You are bent. Your balance is gone. It can't work. You must leave."

"I will fight for my rights, then," hissed Hesperus.

"If you fight, you will lose," cautioned Good One. "Please turn back to the way you were in the beginning when we were all happy."

"No, I will fight!" insisted Hesperus.

And so a great war took place in R-dor. The king's army fought and forced Hesperus and his angels into submission.

"Please, please, do not destroy us," pleaded Hesperus to the king. "If you destroy us, what kind of a loving king does that make you look like? You don't look very good, oh, Good One. Besides, I'm sure my ways will work if you just give me a chance. Let me try my experiment. Let me have one little piece of your universe to try my ways. Perhaps you could banish me to that new little planet you made. I promise I won't go anywhere else."

Good One nodded sadly. "It is a very costly experiment, Hesperus, but have your way. It's the only way to purge the universe. You are banished to earth."

Chapter 1

The Discovery

The weather was warm and tempting. The smell of ripe blackberries perfumed the air. It was a perfect day for riding bikes. Larry and Dave rode to their favorite haunt at City Park. It was a forested ravine at the edge of the large park where the paths had turned to dirt. There it was . . . their old jump spot. The well-worn path shot straight down the hill to a hump that was camouflaged by the contour of the ground and bushes. Beyond the hump, the path widened, dipped to the bottom of the ravine, and continued up the other side into a grove of trees.

Larry hesitated as if unsure of himself. "Want to go first?"

"Sure," Dave replied. In a flash he sped down the hill. A moment later, he and his airborne bike flew over the hump. His landing was great. As he started up the other side, he braked the bike into a skid, and turned around to watch his friend try his wings.

"It's still in good shape!" Dave called out. He watched his friend speeding down the hill, and then laughed as Larry flew off the jump, his face contorted as he pretended to be afraid of this scary maneuver. He skidded to a stop nearby. They grinned at each other.

"Want to go again?" Larry pushed his bike forward and then halted suddenly. Something strange caught his eye. An eerie light glowed from under a large maple leaf. He had never seen anything like that before, and a small chill ran down his spine. "What's that?" he whispered, dropping his bike. He squatted beside the leaf and slowly picked it up, tossing it aside. There lay a small glowing green case.

Dave watched as Larry gingerly touched the golden letters etched into the top. ORB-6, whatever that meant. Larry felt a tingling sensation in his fingers just as Dave shouted, "Watch out!"

Larry jumped and jerked his hand away while Dave laughed in amusement.

"It's probably something the leprechauns forgot on St. Patrick's Day! Open it up. See what's inside," Dave coaxed.

"Are you kidding?" Larry scoffed. "This thing freaks me out! It makes my arm tingle. It's going bye-bye!" Suddenly, he kicked at the case with all his might. It flew off the ground and into the forest.

"Hey, are you crazy man?" Dave shouted disgustedly. "I want to see what's inside. You are such a wimp sometimes!"

"Then go find it for yourself," Larry snorted. "I'm not interested."

"I will," Dave galloped off in the direction the case had landed. "Aren't you the least bit curious why it glows? It could be from outer space or, or, or . . ."

"Or what?" Larry quizzed. He followed his friend, tormenting him.

"Or whatever," Dave mumbled as he continued to search for the case. "I just wanted to see it for myself."

"It could be radioactive," Larry searched for excuses to soothe his fears. He followed reluctantly while Dave searched among the bushes and vines. "I tell you, that thing is spooky."

"Aha!" Dave cried in triumph as he picked up the green case. "Here it is." A look of astonishment crossed his face as he felt the tingling in his arm. "Sheesh! I see what you mean, but I'm not going to be a chicken like you! Here goes a real *man.*" He grinned mischievously and lifted the lid.

Both boys peered curiously at the contents: a pair of unusual green eyeglasses. A glow hovered over them, and the lenses appeared as a cloudy prism, turning different colors as they caught the light. "These are strange-looking glasses." Dave gathered his courage and gently touched them. An exhilarating feeling pulsed through his body.

"I dare you to try them on," Larry goaded his friend. "You'd look like a real stud in those!"

Dave picked up the glasses and let its case fall to the ground. As he put the glasses to his eyes, he was amazed. There were all the normal things he saw without the glasses, but in addition, he saw a mysterious figure standing nearby, looking intently at him. "Yikes," Dave yelled, trying to keep his voice from trembling. "Who are you?"

"Don't be afraid. I am D-go (pronounced Dee-go)," the person in a golden bodysuit shrugged and smiled at him. His eyes were warm and friendly. A red heart glowed from his forehead. Tousled dark hair framed his face. "I am an angel from the kingdom of R-dor on the planet Orb. I won't harm you. I have been sent by our good king to give you these glasses. My job is to protect you and help you, so don't be afraid."

"So why did my arm tingle when I touched the glasses?" Dave's breathing was still a bit rapid.

"It's just the strength from our king going into your body so you can see through the glasses," D-go explained. "The tingling has gone away now, hasn't it?"

Dave nodded, "I was afraid I might grow another head, or start glowing green or something."

D-go chuckled, "No, no, no! It's nothing like that. The glasses will help you see how we angels help you with life. And I've got a special message to give you. You are about to start on a journey to freedom. Our king, Good One, knows you are trapped in a situation at home. He has sent me to help you out of your prison."

Dave felt his knees getting weak. How did this mysterious creature know about the secret horrors of his home? It was like a prison when he was there. He left it to be with Larry as much as he could. The happy times with his friend seemed to ease those terrible secrets of home.

D-go touched Dave sympathetically on the shoulder and continued talking. "Good One wants you to know how much he cares for you. Now, you'll be able to see and talk to those of us who live in the fifth dimension. We are with you all the time, but you just can't see us without this gift." He pointed to the glasses.

Dave's fears began to melt away as he listened to D-go. Larry, who could not see or hear D-go, listened anxiously to Dave's voice and wondered who he was talking to. "What's happening?" his voice trembled. "Are you going insane?"

Dave grinned and reassured Larry. "I'm very fine. I'm having an interesting conversation with someone from another planet! You're missing all the excitement."

"You're putting me on!" Larry replied.

Through the glasses, Dave saw D-go smiling at him. "Tell your fearful friend that maybe he'll be brave enough to talk to my friend and me." He motioned to another being that stood beside him.

Just then, feeling very brave, Larry said, "Let me have a look. I found the glasses first!"

"Oh, all right," Dave responded. "I'm glad you changed your mind." He gently removed the glasses and handed them to his friend. He tried to explain his conversation with D-go to Larry. But he felt so excited, he was sure his words made little sense.

Larry was dumbfounded as he looked through the lenses. Two strangers, D-go and another being, stood nearby.

"I'm L-mor (pronounced El-more)," said the short fat angel with jolly eyes. The red heart in his forehead and golden bodysuit made him look similar to D-go. "Don't be afraid. I've been sent by Good One, our king, to show you how we protect you from harm. It will help you overcome your fear. You remember how just moments ago, you were afraid to even try on these glasses. But Good One knows how brave you would like to be. With the strength of our king, you will be amazed when he awakens the courage that is now asleep in your soul."

Larry was not so sure, and his courage disappeared when he saw some other beings sitting under a tree some distance away. They were dressed in camouflage bodysuits. A large colored patch was attached to the front. Each wore a leather backpack. They sat in the shadows and talked in subdued tones, glaring toward the boys from time to time.

Larry felt a sense of fear, as if those beings were plotting something evil. He shuddered as he turned to L-mor, "Who are those spooky guys over there?"

A sad look passed over L-mor's face. "They're our enemy angels. They're the ones responsible for the bad things that happen everywhere. But D-go and I are here to help you understand the difference between good and evil, so you can choose the best path. Our world plays an important part in your world, yet most people don't realize it because they can't see it. With ORB, you will see."

Larry nodded.

"So we would like to be your friends and journey with you," L-mor paused. "If you keep these glasses, you'll have adventures more exciting than you've ever imagined! We can fly without an airplane and do jumps without a bike! Are you interested in having these glasses?" L-mor asked.

"I think so," Larry hesitated and turned to his friend. "Dave, shall we keep these glasses?" Slowly they nodded. They weren't sure where the glasses would lead them, but it did seem like an unusual adventure.

"You can return these at any time if you change your mind," L-mor told him. "They must be guarded very carefully," he emphasized. "If they get into the wrong hands, they could be destroyed or used by the evil angels. Our enemies over there in the shadows try to destroy all ORBs. They don't like humans seeing the evil tactics they use to influence people. They may pull tricks by using people you trust. Or they may lie to you in order to get the glasses. Never trust those bad angels, or the people on their side." He paused to see if Larry understood his words.

Just then, Larry noticed a movement, and two angels from the shadows appeared. Both wore yellow patches shaped like arrowheads on the front of their camouflage suits.

"Hello, I'd like to meet you," one spoke. His face looked hard and severe. A sly smile played at his lips. He held out his hand.

"What tricks are you up to, Gemini?" L-mor stepped in front of Larry and stared intently at the newcomer.

"I just thought I'd warn these two humans about *your* tricks," Gemini replied, winking at his companion. "What kind of rubbish are you dumping on these poor souls today?"

"That will be enough!" D-go chimed in. "You are the one with the backpack of tricks. Leave at once!" He snapped his fingers together, and the two were flung backward into the woods.

"We're sorry for the interruption," L-mor apologized, shaking his head.

"I don't understand what just happened," Larry puzzled. "Why are they your enemies?"

"It's a long story," L-mor sighed. "But briefly, there was war in our kingdom a long time ago. Hesperus and his followers were banished from R-dor to earth. So they try to get even with Good One by tricking humans to choose their side instead of our king's."

"And you want us to choose your king's side?" Larry questioned.

L-mor nodded and then spoke. "Everyone chooses between the good or evil kingdoms, whether they realize it or not. Our king is very different from Hesperus. With the glasses, you can see for yourself and make your own choice." He paused to see if Larry understood.

Larry was puzzled about L-mor's words about choosing a kingdom. He was not aware that choosing kingdoms were part of his home, school, or life!

L-mor sensed the hesitation and reassured Larry. "In time you will understand. Just try the glasses for yourself. Let me show you how they work." He pointed to two buttons on ORB, one on either side of the frames. "When something happens to you that you don't understand, push this button." He pointed to the arrow button with the initials RW. "It will replay your past in the fifth dimension. When you are worried about the future, press this arrow button called FF. It will be a big help, but use it sparingly. The future belongs to our king, not to humans. Why don't you try the buttons?"

Larry sat on the ground and motioned for his friend, Dave, to sit beside him. He explained what L-mor had told him. "I'm going to try out these buttons now." He pushed the RW button. Immediately, the lenses in the glasses split into two screens. On one screen, he saw the present scene around him with his angel L-mor standing at his side. But the other screen went back in time and played his past life as if he were on television. He saw himself riding his bike with Dave to the park. He saw himself pausing at the top of the hill while Dave got ready to go down the jump. He was surprised to see two of the angels in camouflage suits dart from the shadows and push a rock down the hill so that it landed in the path right below the bike jump. Soon Dave would be flying down the hill, not knowing the rock and danger were there. But then he saw L-mor and D-go skimming over the ground ahead of Dave, pushing the rock out of the way. Dave whizzed by seconds later, a grin on his face, oblivious that a rock had ever been in his path. Then he saw himself following his friend down the bike-run.

Larry pushed the RW button again to stop the picture. He turned to L-mor and spoke with an awed tone. "Wow, I had no idea. Thanks, L-mor and D-go, for keeping us safe! Now I'm going to test the FF button on ORB." Through the split screen in the glasses, he watched as he and Dave started for home, their golden angels close by. He also noticed the enemy angels studying them carefully from a distance and then disappearing instantly.

"Be on your guard!" warned L-mor. "Ride carefully. Our enemies are at work."

Chapter 2

The Enemy

Larry and Dave looked at each other as if to say, "What's next?" The secluded area of the park had witnessed their secret discovery.

"Who gets to keep these?" asked Larry as he tucked the green glasses in their case.

"I think you should," Dave mused out loud. "If my dad should ever find them at our house, they would be history."

Larry understood. He put the green case in his shirt pocket. They fit, but the eerie glow shone from the top of the pocket. "Do you think I should tell anyone about the glasses, like my parents or our friends?"

"They'd probably think you were crazy," Dave shared. "And besides, if what L-mor told us is true, it will be easier for the enemy angels to get ORB away from us if more people know about it."

"That's true, so let's keep ORB a secret until we understand a little more about it," Larry reasoned. "I have lots of questions about the angels, but we don't have time to ask them now. Our parents will be wondering where we are." He patted his pocket to make sure the glasses were still there. "At home, I can keep these in the back of my computer desk drawer until we figure out a safer place for them."

"The sooner we get them there, the better. It's not much of a secret that there's something weird in that pocket!" Dave pointed to the obvious bulge in Larry's shirt.

The boys pushed their bikes out of the ravine and cautiously entered the open area of the park. Larry's eyes spanned the horizon from one end to the other as he commented, "L-mor's last words were 'Be on your guard!' So be my cover. I think we might have trouble on our way home."

Dave took the lead. He saw that it was safe to ride through the park without attracting much attention. The boys mounted their bikes and pedaled with purpose to the park exit, and into the side streets that led to Larry's home. The boys felt pretty well protected here. It was an older residential section of Warrenville, their town. Lots of tall trees and hedges around the houses blocked the view of any casual onlooker.

The boys let down their guard a bit, and increased their speed. Just then, a car came from behind and turned into the street they were planning to take. They quickly steered onto the sidewalk instead. As they rounded the corner they were surprised to find three girls directly in their path. The boys frantically braked and tried to stop their bikes or veer to the side. Instead they and their bikes skidded and crashed in disarray on the sidewalk in front of the indignant girls.

"Watch where you're going!" shouted Winnie, the redheaded, freckle-faced girl. Gray eyes glared through the round lenses of her thick glasses. "You almost ran us down! Can't you see we're on our way to a party? You almost got our nice clothes messed up. And if you had ruined these gifts, I'd have made you pay for everything."

"Sorry," muttered Larry. He rubbed a scraped elbow and tried to get back on his feet. It was then that he noticed that ORB had fallen from his pocket. Hastily, he picked it up from the sidewalk. He tried to slip it back into his pocket without being noticed. But Winnie's sharp eyes caught the movement.

"What's that?" Winnie's eyes narrowed, her words hissed through the wide space between her front teeth. She pointed to the bulge in Larry's pocket. "I bet you stole it! Or maybe it's drugs," she accused.

By this time, the boys were mounting their bikes, hoping for a speedy escape, but Winnie jumped in front of Larry, hands on hips, blocking his exit. "What's in your pocket?" she demanded again.

"None of your business!" responded Larry.

Winnie's face turned red, and she shook her finger as she bellowed mean and ugly words. Larry finally pushed her aside enough to escape. "Well, never mind, Smarty Pants," Winnie called after him. "I'll just ask your sister, Cheryl. She tells me *everything*!"

The boys scooted away with Winnie's loud insults and threats following them the length of the block. At last it was quiet, and they rode quickly. No one said a word. They were thankful they had gotten away. "I've never liked that girl," Dave said at last.

"Same here," Larry responded. "She's a bully at school, too. I always head another direction if I see her coming! I hate it that she's friends with my sister."

"She always seems to be the ringleader for the troublemakers," Dave commented. "I sure wish she hadn't seen ORB. There's no telling what she'll do with that bit of information!"

"I know," Larry agreed. Their bikes wheeled into the subdivision where Larry lived, just a few blocks from downtown. As they turned into his driveway, the white two-story house greeted them. Large oak trees sprawled in the yard next to the house. "Want to come in for a minute?" Larry asked. "It might be fun to see ORB's version of our incident with Winnie."

"Sure, but I need to get home pretty soon to do chores," Dave said.

The boys slipped through the back door and into the kitchen, where the air was full of good smells. Mrs. Foster, Larry's mother, was busy taking something from the oven. They greeted her quickly, and then headed up the stairs to Larry's room. A hastily made bed stood in one corner of the room. Its brown spread hung a bit askew over slightly rumpled blankets and sheets. Tiger, the gray-striped cat, was nestled like a ball, fast asleep against the hump where the pillow lay. The remains of Larry's clothes from yesterday lay on the floor near the closet where they had been tossed the night before. A couple of chairs sat near the desk, sitting just as they were last used. The light green walls were decorated with posters of baseball heroes. A plastic bin near the closet door contained a collection of rackets, bats, balls, and miscellaneous gear. Light from the window filtered through the leaves of the oak tree outside onto Larry's wooden desk. It was cluttered with school papers, a computer, and other treasures. This was a comfortable room. Larry and his best friend Dave had spent many an hour here, talking, playing games, and enjoying each other's company.

Safely behind the closed door, Larry removed ORB from his pocket. He carefully examined it again. The soft glow no longer worried him. He fitted the glasses over his eyes. Pushing the rewind button, he was shocked to see the accident that had happened a few minutes before with Winnie and her friends.

"Can you believe it!" Larry exclaimed. "The bad angels are shooting dart guns at all of us! They're telling Winnie everything to say! She's repeating everything she hears from them! No wonder L-mor warned us to beware. He and D-go are catching all the darts aimed at us, and they're telling us to get away as quickly as possible!"

Larry gave the glasses to Dave so he could see for himself. "This is hard to believe," Dave mused as he watched the replay.

"I know it must seem that way to you," D-go, the angel beside him interjected.

"What's with the dart gun and darts the enemy is using?" Dave wanted to know.

"The poisoned darts are aimed at the mind," D-go answered. "When a dart hits anyone, it injects evil and mean thoughts into the mind unless it is removed quickly. That's how fights get started."

Dave was puzzled. "I don't understand why they hate us so much. We haven't done anything to them."

"They hate you because you are precious to our king. It hurts Good One to see his children tortured, so that's how Hesperus gets even with him. The evil angels capture you by playing mind games with the darts. But Good One captures our hearts with his love so we can have freedom. We'll talk more about it as we become better friends."

"Okay," Dave said thoughtfully, not sure he understood what D-go meant by "capturing" "mind games" and "freedom."

"Speaking of freedom, I have something for you." D-go pulled a metal piece from his pocket and held it toward Dave. The object looked like a framework of a small house, but little bars with knobs covered the surface, making it look like a bumpy cage. It was attached to a silver chain.

"This is called a k-sun," D-go explained. "It's a symbol of your journey to freedom. As we go along together, events will occur that will mark your progress, and we will add pieces to your little prison to make it into something beautiful. It will be a prized treasure for you always. Wear it around your neck so you can keep it near your heart."

Dave looked down at the little object in his hand. It was a reminder of the secret prison he lived in. He was ashamed of his situation, so ashamed that he talked to no one about it. Yet, D-go was giving him something that continually reminded him he was trapped. He couldn't think of anything to say. Finally he mumbled, "This is heavy for its size!"

D-go smiled, "That way, you'll notice it more as you wear it. In Good One's wise time you will understand as you get more pieces for this."

"Okay," Dave shrugged. "I'll talk to you again soon." He removed ORB, placed it back in its case, and gave it to Larry. Carefully he slipped the k-sun over his head. It hung next to his heart.

Suddenly there was a knock at the door. Larry gasped inwardly as he heard his sister's voice. He did not want Cheryl, of all people, to discover ORB. Here it was, glowing in his hand.

"Just a minute!" Larry called out, desperately wondering what to do with the secret glasses. Quickly he opened his top computer desk drawer, and tossed ORB in the hidden compartment at the back.

He could hear Cheryl whining through the door. "Why all the secrecy? I just need to borrow your baseball glove."

Larry shut the desk drawer with one sweeping motion, and called, "Well, come in." The door swung open, and Cheryl sauntered over to the bin of rackets, bats, and balls.

"Well?" Cheryl raised her eyebrows questioningly.

"You want to borrow it *again*?" complained Larry, "You just used it yesterday." It seemed like she used the mitt more than he did these days. "Well, okay," he finally agreed, "but be sure to return it today."

"I will!" Cheryl retorted. Her pretty blue eyes sparked with impatience. Her body language betrayed annoyance as she grabbed the glove from Larry's bin and rushed out the door and down the stairs.

"That was a close one," Larry drew a deep breath. "She almost caught us!"

"I know," Dave replied. "I tried to look cool, but I didn't feel that way! Well, I'd better get home. See you at school tomorrow! It's been an interesting day . . ."

Larry had a hard time going to sleep that night. When he finally dropped off, he was bothered with nightmares. He dreamt he was in shop class. The teacher was insisting that they learn to pound a nail into a block of wood. In his dream the technique was complicated, and the teacher kept getting on his case for not doing it right. He had to pound his nail over and over and over. Other kids were pounding their nails over and over and over. The pounding became louder and louder and louder, until he woke up with a start.

He could hear a rapping noise. It sounded like someone was tapping on his window. How could that be? His room was on the second floor of the house. He looked toward the window, and in the darkness, he saw a shadowy figure, half clinging to the oak tree outside and half poised against his window. Who was trying to break into his room?

Chapter 3

The Legions

Larry could hear his heart pounding in his head. Who was trying to break into his room in the middle of the night? He jumped out of bed, thinking he would make a dash to his folk's room, when he heard a faint voice calling his name. The voice sounded vaguely familiar.

"Larry, it's me. Let me in," Cheryl called to him, hoping no one else heard.

Larry sighed, scuffled to the window, and opened it. "Whatever are you doing out here?"

She pulled herself through the window and whispered. "I snuck out the back door. I was hungry for a milk shake, so went down to Dairy Queen. When I got back, the door had been locked. I didn't want to wake up Mom and Dad, so I decided to climb your tree. You won't tell on me, will you?"

"You silly sister," Larry scolded as he looked at his clock. It was 11:30 p.m. "Don't you know you could have been kidnapped or picked up by some riffraff? You could have fallen from that tree?"

"But I didn't," Cheryl whispered saucily. "So please, please, please don't tell on me. I'll buy you a milk shake."

"Oh, just get out of here," Larry quipped with annoyance. He shut the door softly behind her and then the window. "Sisters," he muttered to himself as he tiptoed back to bed.

* * *

The sun glistened through the trees when Larry and Cheryl boarded the bus for school the next morning. He and Dave attended ninth grade in the high school across town, and Cheryl attended junior high in the adjoining building.

Larry was still thinking about ORB, and what the angels might be doing at this moment. He would have to check that out tonight when he got home. In the meantime, ORB was safely hidden in his computer desk.

The bus lumbered slowly along the city streets, picking up students at the designated stops. When they got to the corner near Dave's house, a sleepy-looking Dave climbed aboard and plopped down on the seat beside Larry.

"Are you okay?" questioned Larry.

"Uh-huh," responded Dave. "Sort of . . . well . . . I didn't get a lot of sleep last night. My dad was drinking, and he got me up in the middle of the night to finish chores he thought I should have done."

"I'm sorry," comforted Larry, noticing a red mark across Dave's face. He knew Mr. Lister, Dave's dad, must have beaten him again. Poor Dave.

There was an awkward silence, but then the bus door was opening. They had arrived at school. The boys milled their way through the mixed crowd to their homeroom. They couldn't help noticing a satisfied gleam in Winnie's eyes as they passed her in the hall. Her nose rose a little higher in the air as she clomped off.

They'd only been in class a short time, when Larry was summoned to go to the school principal's office. Mr. Stern was a serious-faced, bald man with bushy eyebrows that shaded his thick, black-rimmed glasses. He stared at a paper clenched between his two hands. "I've had a report that we must deal with here," he opened the conversation. "It says here that you were trying to sell drugs to other students. Where were you yesterday?" He peered over his paper at Larry with beady, laserlike eyes.

Larry hesitated, collecting his thoughts and trying not to let those laser eyes frighten him. He trembled inside and replied nervously, "I was home except for a few hours when I rode my bike in the park."

"Were you with anyone?"

"My friend Dave and I rode together."

"Who did you talk to in the park?" the principal probed.

"Just Dave. No one else." Larry was *not* going to tell the principal about his conversation with angels!

"Who did you talk to on the way home?" the principal questioned again.

"Only some girls we almost ran into. We had a close call," Larry offered.

"What were you carrying in your pocket—a green case that you apparently didn't want anyone to see?"

"Oh, nothing much, just something personal. It wasn't drugs or anything." Larry hoped fear did not show in his eyes. Then a sense of peace floated over him. He had done nothing wrong, he told himself. Punishment was only for those who had done wrong. He would be safe.

"You're sure?" Mr. Stern quipped, his voice rising. "We can't be too careful. We don't want any drug dealing around this school." In a severe voice, he added, "Let me warn you that the consequences of selling drugs are mighty serious. It's a crime!" His eyes narrowed as he stared at Larry. It seemed as if those eyes would pierce right through him. "I'm warning you! I'll be keeping an eye on you." With a nod toward the door he added, "You may go."

Larry was seldom brave enough to try anything against the rules, and so had never been in trouble at school. This incident was embarrassing and maddening. He knew that Winnie had been at the bottom of all of it, but he collected himself and tried to appear unshaken when he returned to his desk. Dave gave him a questioning look. "Winnie's tricks," Larry whispered. "I'll tell you later."

Larry found it hard to concentrate on the literature assignment. His gaze shifted aimlessly around the room. His eyes rested on a skinny boy, Todd, who was staring out the window. Todd was a loner. He didn't take part in class activities or respond much to any efforts the guys made to become acquainted. It was as if he was becoming invisible. People were noticing him less and less. He just came to school, sat in his desk, and then went home.

Then Larry shifted his gaze to the opposite side of the room. There was the new girl; he thought her name was Jodi. She had short, bobbed brown hair that shone like her soft brown eyes did. She was busy writing on her paper. Her eyes lifted and caught Larry's gaze. She smiled and turned back to her work. Larry also looked down at his book. "I think she's kind of cute," he thought to himself for a fleeting moment. But then the bell rang, and it was time to move on to science class.

As the boys moved into the hall, Larry turned to Dave with a subdued tone. "I got turned in to the principal. He was giving me a hard time for selling drugs, and asked me about the green case. It had to be Winnie's fault. She must have come up with a real tall tale to tell the principal."

Dave nodded. "What did you tell him?" he asked with concern.

"I told him it was not drugs, and was just something personal. And he seemed okay with that, but afterward he gave me a big lecture about selling drugs being a crime. I hope that's the end of that. He said he'd be watching me."

"That Winnie is a witch!" Dave fumed.

After school, Dave rode the bus to Larry's home. Both were anxious to see ORB's version of the morning's scene. They found the door to Larry's room ajar. The top desk drawer was slightly opened.

A look of concern passed between the boys. Was ORB safe? Quietly, they closed the door and approached the desk. Pulling the desk drawer out a little further, Larry opened the secret compartment and breathed a sigh of relief. ORB was glowing gently from its hiding place. Then Larry saw a note on the top of his desk. It was scribbled in his sister's handwriting: "I've borrowed your glove again. Thanks!"

"That explains it," Larry whispered thoughtfully. "She left the drawer open when hunting for a pencil. Too close for comfort, I'd say!"

Carefully, Larry opened ORB's case and put the glasses on. Touching the rewind button, he watched the morning's events as they entered the school building. There were so many good and bad angels there. When Winnie passed in the hall, she was looking pleased with herself. Several angels in camouflage crowded around her, slapping her on the back and complimenting her on the good job she had done. They seemed to be pleased with themselves and Winnie.

L-mor stood by Larry's side, "I'll be with you," he encouraged.

Next Larry saw himself being called to the principal's office. He could hear the evil angels chuckling wickedly, but L-mor brushed them aside with a quick motion of his arm. L-mor's presence strengthened Larry, as he faced Mr. Stern. One evil angel continued ridiculing him, and another hovered around Mr. Stern, suggesting accusations and conclusions to make. Darts were zooming toward Mr. Stern. Suddenly, two more angels with hearts in their foreheads appeared and intercepted some of the darts. They removed others that had landed on Mr. Stern's head. Then they pushed away the evil angel beside Mr. Stern, and positioned themselves behind the desk on either side of the principal. They smiled at Larry, and then leaned forward, crossing their arms back and forth.

"Hey," said Larry excitedly to Dave, as he realized what the angels were doing. "The angels from Good One's kingdom were giving me the 'safe' signal that an ump uses at a baseball game! That must have been when I started feeling that everything would work out okay."

Larry continued watching as he made his way back to class. He saw L-mor beside him. As the evil angel whispered thoughts of shame and discouragement to Larry, L-mor intervened. "Leave him alone, Scorpio!" he said, snapping his fingers together. The evil angel was immediately flung against the wall, disappearing through it as if by magic. "Enough is enough," L-mor commented quietly to Larry.

When Larry returned to his homeroom and sat down at his desk, he noticed angels hovering nearby. They kept a watchful eye on each person. But there were several angels in camouflage gathered around Todd. They were continually sending negative messages to him. They told him no one liked him, he was ugly, and all his classmates were bad. As Todd listened to the negative messages, the evil angels wrapped dark strands of thread around his body. One could see he was slowly being paralyzed by the webs they were spinning around him. An angel from Good One's kingdom was giving him messages, too, telling him not to listen to the bad messages, as they were not true. They wanted to free Todd from the strands, and looked to Todd for permission to do that. But Todd paid no attention to them. He was listening to the evil angels.

Then Larry noticed an orange arrowhead patch on a bad angel's chest. Other angels wore yellow, red, green, and other colored patches. "Who's the angel with the orange patch?" Larry asked L-mor.

"That's Leo, the leader of a legion. Hesperus, who is the leader of the evil angels, has organized his army in groups called legions. One legion has one job and wears its colored badge, and others wear another color. Leo's group is called the Revenge Legion. He tries to get wars started and encourages violence. There are hundreds of different legions, each trying in their own way to pull down humans so that they no longer have the strength and courage to choose what is good and right. Are you beginning to understand how Hesperus and his angels work?"

Larry nodded.

"And do you understand why they are our enemies?"

Larry nodded again. He turned his attention to more of the morning's events playing out in the lenses of ORB. An evil angel hovered over Jodi. It was watching everything she did, and whispered words to her from time to time. "What legion does that angel by Jodi belong to?" asked Larry.

"He belongs to the Devaluation Legion," said L-mor.

"And what legion does Scorpio belong to?" asked Larry.

"He belongs to the Discouragement Legion." L-mor saw the worried expression on Larry's face. He continued, "Never fear. Be of good courage. Good One's son is our commander. His name is Guerdon, and he is stronger than all the forces of Hesperus. He could zap them all into oblivion if he wanted. But Good One is giving time to humans so they can choose whose side they want to be on. He will know when the time is right to stop the war."

L-mor opened his hand and showed Larry a small metal object attached to a chain. "This is your k-sun. Perhaps Dave showed his to you yesterday. But your quest is different. It is to find courage. Today you experienced a frightening event. Did you learn anything from it?" L-mor's soft eyes searched Larry's face for a response.

Larry thought for a moment, and then it came to him. "You helped me through it! I survived! I did not get punished!"

L-mor smiled broadly. "That's it! That's the first step in your quest for courage. Knowing that *we are with you* will help you in every scary experience you get into. So here's the first piece to attach to your k-sun."

Larry looked at his k-sun. Its small knobby wires were shaped like a little fort. He took the shiny silver piece that L-mor had and tried to attach it.

"It has to go on the foundation of the fort," L-mor suggested. The piece clicked easily into place.

Dave moved closer to look at Larry's k-sun. "Cool! When you get through with ORB, I'd like to have a turn."

"Oh, sure." Larry removed the glasses and gave them carefully to Dave.

When Dave pressed the RW button, the scene before him was the dreaded experience of the night before. He saw the evil angel bombarding his drunken father with black darts. Driven by that angel, Mr. Lister rushed to awaken Dave. He yanked Dave from bed and pushed him to the kitchen, where he had discovered some dirty dishes in the sink. As the dark darts hit Mr. Lister's head, he listened intently to the suggestions of the evil angel. He got more and more angry. Dave winced again, and tears welled up in his eyes as he watched his father striking him. Then he saw his protective angel, D-go, coming between his father and him. His dad punched D-go in the shoulder without realizing it. A confused look crossed his father's face, and he turned around and stomped off. When Dave returned to his room and curled up in bed, he saw tears spilling from D-go's eyes as he rubbed his shoulder. He then cradled Dave's head in his lap and whispered encouraging words to him.

"Thank you for helping me, D-go," Dave murmured softly. "You were with me there."

"Yes, I am always with you, and things will work out for you someday." D-go patted Dave's shoulder and handed him a shiny silver piece. "This is for realizing I am with you. Fit it in the foundation of your k-sun." Dave snapped the piece on one of the knobs.

"Why does my dad drink so much?" Dave wanted to know.

D-go responded softly, "That evil angel you saw works for the Addiction Legion, and they've almost got your dad trapped in their web. You saw the dark strands of webs wrapped around him. Without the help of Good One and his spirit, he'll never be free."

"What do you mean, 'spirit'?" asked Dave.

"It's another one of Good One's family. We call him Zephyr," explained D-go. "His presence is like the soft winds that cover the whole earth, and he encourages people to choose Good One's kingdom. We all help each other and the earthlings."

When the boys were through talking to L-mor and D-go, they carefully put ORB back in its case. Larry returned it to its hiding place at the back of his desk drawer. Just then, a gray fluffy object landed on the windowsill. It was Tiger, Larry's cat. He liked to leap from the tree outside into Larry's room.

"Hello, you old purr-bag," Larry greeted him. He scratched the tabby cat under his chin. Tiger jumped onto the desk and rubbed his head, and then his whole body against Larry. Tiger's body seemed to vibrate with the loud rumble of his purr. "Hey, quit slobbering on me!" Larry laughed, as he wiped his hand on his pants.

The distant voice of Larry's mother drifted into the room from below. "Supper time. Come get it!"

"I'd better get home now," said Dave. I'll see you tomorrow.

* * *

After the evening meal, Larry joined his dad, who was watching TV in the family room. Larry admired his dad and trusted his wise counsel and support.

"How was your day, son?"

"Well," Larry hesitated, as he chose his words carefully. "I think I'd better tell you what happened today at school before you hear it from someone else. I got called in to the principal's office."

"Yes?" Larry had Dad's full attention.

"Well, I think the story began yesterday when I almost ran into some girls with my bike. I crashed to the ground and some stuff fell out of my pocket. No one got hurt except for my skinned elbow. But this girl was mad and accused me of having drugs. She's not very nice, and totally wrong about the drugs. But today, the principal asked me if I was doing drugs, and gave me a big lecture about it. I think Winnie tried to get me in trouble."

"Hmmm," Mr. Foster responded. "Was that Mr. Stern that talked to you?"

"Yes, and Winnie is the girl that Cheryl hung out with some last year."

"Yes, I remember Winnie," Mr. Foster shook his head knowingly. "Thanks for telling me about this, son. I know it was a hard experience for you, and hopefully, nothing more will come of this. If it does, let's keep talking. I'll support you all the way."

"Thanks," Larry realized how much he really appreciated his dad. "I guess I'd better do some homework, now. See you later!"

Chapter 4

The Rally of Light

Larry felt a sandpaper tongue licking his cheek. "Tiger, leave me alone!" he protested. He turned over and buried his face in the pillow, but he could not shut out the loud rumble that continued six inches from his head. He felt a soft paw touch his ear, as if to say, "Wake up, buddy. I'd like my breakfast *now*!"

Larry looked at the clock. It was 6:45 a.m. "Okay, purr-bag," he mumbled. "You always get your own way around here." He stretched and rolled out of bed. As soon as Larry's feet touched the floor, the cat began meowing urgently and pacing toward the door. The meow chorus lasted all the while they walked down the stairs and into the utility room where the cat food and Tiger's dish were kept. "There, Tiger. I hope you're satisfied," Larry talked to the cat as if he understood every word he was saying. Tiger just continued to purr, only pausing a moment with each swallow of food. He glanced up at Larry from time to time, just to make sure he was still there.

With this morning ritual over, Larry paused to greet his mother who was making breakfast in the kitchen, and then returned to his room to get ready for the day. As he entered his room, his eyes fell on the computer desk. There was his silvery k-sun on top, and ORB was safely hidden inside. He felt a strong urge to talk to his angel, to be prepared for the day. Quietly, he opened the drawer wide, removed the green case, and put the glasses in place.

"You heard me calling you," L-mor greeted him with a big smile. "I wanted to tell you that the angels are having a rally of light tonight at 7:00 p.m. at the school football field. You are invited to come."

"Sounds interesting," Larry responded, wondering how he could work out the details with his folks so as not to arouse suspicion. "Thanks for the invite." He knew something would work out.

* * *

The sun was low in the sky as Larry and Dave made their way to a bleacher on the edge of the football field. It would soon be dark and the air cool. Not a soul was in sight. Carefully, Larry removed ORB from his pocket and put the glasses in place. The sudden light through the lenses blinded him, and he shut his eyes for an instant. Adjusting to the glowing circle of light, he saw the football field full of bright angels. The sound of their excited voices bubbled with expectancy. L-mor was nearby, and he glowed from top to bottom. Around the edges of the gathering, Larry saw the black angels, trying to work their way into the circle, but there were guards of bright angels stationed around the parameter of the circle, protecting those inside from the attacks of the evil ones. Now and again there were commotions along the border, as the evil ones tried to make their way inside, but they did not succeed.

"The program is about to begin," L-mor informed him. "Watch carefully." Then, as if a timed signal had been given, the angels all snapped their fingers simultaneously. Instantly, the dark angels were flung away from the group like rockets launched into orbit.

Larry noticed that some of the angels did not glow with the light as L-mor did, and they appeared dejected. But the glowing angels gently and playfully pushed them into the center of the circle. Larry recognized Winnie's protective angel and his classmate Todd's angel. "What's happening?" Larry asked L-mor. "Why do these angels not glow?"

"These angels are sad and downhearted," L-mor replied, "because their *kananas* (that's what we call the people we are assigned to protect) are making bad choices, and it's putting them in the enemy's territory. See how these angels will be strengthened for their hard tasks."

Larry shared the ORB with Dave so he could see this amazing rally. "There's the angel that cares for my dad," Dave noticed. "They're pushing him to the center!"

Just then, a shining creature carrying a golden bowl flew above the angels. The creature was as bright as the sunshine, and a crown sparkled from its head. It had many arms that waved about. Playfully, it pretended to drop the bowl and catch it again with another arm in midair. The contents of the bowl almost spilled out, but not quite. The unique being flew in circles, performing flying stunts with the bowl, tossing it about, and each time catching it again. All onlookers smiled as they watched the aerobatic antics of this being that they all seemed to know and trust. Then a melodious voice rang out. "I carry the bowl of encouragement. Take heart my warriors, and lift your faces up. I sprinkle you with drops from above!" With that, the shining being scattered the contents of the bowl in one amazing swoop, swirling the drops in the shape of a smiley face.

Down, down came millions of glistening drops, spreading out from the giant swirl like golden snowflakes. As the serious angels received the drops on their upturned faces, a glow came over their whole being. A smile came to their faces. But then other angels who were encircling them rushed forward, grabbing the newly glowing angel by the hands and feet, swinging him high into the air. As an angel landed in the arms of others, they called out, "My gift to you is strength!" They playfully swung him to another group, who caught him and called out, "My gift to you is hope!" Over and over again, the angels caught their comrades, giving each one gifts of cheer, courage, patience, trust, and love.

As soft music began, the shiny creature flew above the angels and spread out its many arms, as if to form a giant umbrella. The arms touched each angel, who in turn surrounded one another in a group hug, swaying gently to the time of the music, and singing softly, and then with increasing intensity:

The king we serve is good
His cause is just and true
We will defeat the foe
And this we'll surely do.
And this we'll surely do.

As if by magic, a glimmering golden pillar came out of the ground, and the shining creature came to rest upon it. All could see and hear the words that seemed to come from a big place. "My dear comrades," began the being. "Once upon a time, the Good One we serve planted a special field of grain. But when the seeds began to grow, his helpers noticed that there were many weeds also growing in the field. They discussed this problem with the Good One and realized that an enemy had planted those bad seeds. It was a terrible disappointment. But in his wonderful wisdom, the Good One said to let both the good and the bad seeds grow together until the time of the harvest. When the plants are young, both good and bad plants look very much alike. When they are ripe and ready for harvest, all can tell which are good and which are bad. Then Good One's plants will be saved and the weeds destroyed.

"I know you all understand the meaning of this story. You were there with me in our kingdom, R-dor, when Hesperus planted the bad seeds that turned some of the angels into weeds, and you saw the weeds growing up in our midst. You were there when we helped our commander Guerdon defeat Hesperus and his followers, and banish them from R-dor and the universe. Earth is his last stronghold, and he is planting his bad seeds here as well. He is spreading his darkness. He knows how much that hurts our Good One's family. Hesperus does not fight fairly, but shoots his darts of tricks and lies. He weakens his captives with webs until they cannot think to make right choices. We have the power to defeat the enemy in an instant, but that could cause all who remain to serve the Good One out of fear instead of love. Fear is not the way of our kingdom. Our kingdom is about love, a love beyond anything humans can imagine, a love that creates freedom. His great longing is that our *kananas* choose him because they truly want to, and want to join this circle of love.

"And so I encourage you to persevere and continue your good work of helping your *kanana* understand the war we fight, and know what is right and what is wrong. Remember that the Good One and Guerdon and Zephyr have promised to be with you always. Love conquers all!"

The pillar upon which the speaker stood began to descend, and music swelled up like nothing Larry or Dave had ever heard. A sound similar to a chorus of trumpets began punctuating the music, as if heralding the entrance of nobility. Then all eyes turned upward, as a large dazzling ball descended. It seemed to be made of curved crystal spokes and studded with precious jewels, and inside the ball, one could see a glorious being with a golden crown on his head. He smiled and waved to the crowd. "It's Guerdon, our commander," L-mor shouted with joy. "I must go to him!"

Instantly, the angels joined hands, flying as angel streamers around and over the dazzling ball. Dave wondered how they kept from colliding with one another, but he saw that they flew in perfect pattern with the others, creating designs of beauty as they spun faster and faster, each stream in its own orbit. The angels started singing for the sheer joy of it: "Honor and love and majesty to our king!" Then a higher echo of the song came from others, and still more echoes, with harmony fresh and clear. It was a joyful event for all.

A familiar voice brought the boys back to reality. "What on earth are you doing here, sitting in the dark?" questioned Cheryl, Larry's sister. "Nice light you have there. But Dad's ready to go and has been looking all over for you."

Larry pulled ORB from his eyes as quickly as he could, and pushed them hastily into his jacket pocket. "We're coming!" Larry responded instinctively, hoping that in the darkness, Cheryl would not have noticed *what* was making that light she saw. The boys hurriedly rose to leave, but just had to look back at the dark empty football field, which only moments before had been filled with light and angels and music. Right now, the mighty commander Guerdon must still be the center of attention, but Larry and Dave's human eyes could no longer see or hear the celebration. They hurried along with Cheryl, only half listening to her chatter, as the impact of the rally was still uppermost in their minds.

Chapter 5

The Discovery of ORB

"So where were you boys?" Larry's dad asked as they got into the car. His voice sounded a bit impatient.

"We were just talking out by the football field. There was no one to bother us out there." Larry hoped to sound logical, but Cheryl was rolling her eyes in disbelief. Her quick eyes had noticed the glow. She'd seen Larry's attempts to conceal something that he obviously did not want her or the parents to know about. She loved a good mystery, and she would do her best to solve it. And if it got the boys in trouble, it would be even more fun! She smiled to herself.

Cheryl was a year and a half younger than Larry. Her light brown hair framed a pretty face with sparkling blue eyes, and a nice smile that could warm you up. But she struggled being the younger sister, and tried to be as grown up as Larry. She wanted to play sports with Larry and his friends, and for a girl, she was pretty good at baseball and football. The frustrating thing for Larry was that she had a way of getting what she wanted, sometimes without him realizing what she was doing.

The next Monday at school, Cheryl happened to meet Winnie. "I haven't seen you in ages!" Cheryl greeted her friend. "We used to see each other so often when we were younger and lived in the same neighborhood. How have you been?"

"I'm fine, but getting too old for the Barbie dolls now," Winnie laughed.

"Me, too, believe it or not!" Cheryl replied.

"Say, I've wanted to talk to you," Winnie said, changing the subject, and sidling up to Cheryl as if she were her best friend. Lowering her voice, she whispered, "Your brother has been acting very strange lately. Do you know what he's up to?"

"No, I don't. I've been noticing the same thing," Cheryl said. "He and Dave were all alone out by the football field last night, just sitting in the dark and staring straight ahead. But there was a strange light with them that I don't understand. When I came up, Larry tried to hide something in his pocket. I don't know what it was. It's a mystery to me. What makes you think he's strange?"

Winnie replied too eagerly, "I think it has something to do with the green case that glows," she hissed. "It fell out of Larry's pocket when his bike crashed in front of me last week, and he sure scrambled to hide it from me."

"A green case that glows?" Cheryl questioned. "How big is it?"

Winnie described the case in detail and said, "I'm just dying to know what's so special about that silly green case. Do you suppose Larry keeps it in his room?"

"Well, I'm going to find out!" Cheryl said with the sly grin she wore when she was pleased with her plans.

The next morning, Cheryl complained of not feeling well and asked her mother if she could stay home from school. Cheryl's forlorn face and rapid breathing convinced her mother that it would be best. She felt Cheryl's forehead. "You don't seem to have a fever. Do you think you can stay home by yourself, or should I stay with you?" Mrs. Foster asked tenderly.

"I think I'll be fine alone, Mom," Cheryl whispered sleepily.

Mrs. Foster prepared a sick tray for Cheryl as she was leaving, and placed a phone beside her bed, saying, "Now call me at work if you start feeling worse. I'll be back at noon to check on you." As she left, Mrs. Foster turned at the door and smiled her good-bye.

When the door closed, Cheryl smiled gleefully. Her plan was working out. Her mother was the last one to leave the house that morning, and now the sound of her car disappeared from hearing range. The house was quiet. Cheryl hopped nimbly out of bed and across the hall to Larry's room. As she stood in the doorway, she looked about, wondering where to begin her search. Maybe the closet or the chest of drawers or the desk, she thought. She opened the closet door. There were the games on the shelves, some books, and folded sweatshirts. There was the chest of drawers, and she opened the top drawer . . . underwear . . . she closed that drawer quickly and went to the next. Drawer by drawer, she peeked and closed each one until she got to the bottom. There were miscellaneous things in that drawer—batteries, belts, a wallet, a squirt gun, and small boxes of cancelled stamps for a stamp collection. After examining this drawer more carefully, Cheryl closed it. She didn't see a small green case as Winnie had described, so she turned to the desk.

Tiger lay sleeping, sprawled on top of the desk despite the papers and pencils underneath him. He squinted at Cheryl sleepily as she approached the desk, and then closed his eyes again. Cheryl opened the top drawer, but saw nothing. However, with her detective eyes, she noticed that the drawer did not seem to open very far. She felt the back of the drawer and realized it was a covered compartment. How would she get into it? Her heart beat faster, as she realized that she was on to something.

She was startled by the phone ringing in her bedroom. Impatiently, she hurried to get the phone. It was mother, so she'd better answer it. Putting on her sick, sleepy voice, she answered, "Hello."

"Sorry to disturb you, dear," Mrs. Foster said, "but I forgot to tell you that the tree removal company should be coming by today to trim the trees along the driveway and remove the one in the back. They may be a bit noisy, but there should be no need for them to come into the house for anything."

"Okay," Cheryl replied.

"Are you feeling any better?" asked her mother.

"I'm not sure. Maybe," Cheryl said weakly, trying to play the part.

"Well, get a good rest, and I'll see you at noon," Mrs. Foster advised. "Bye!"

Cheryl put down the phone, and breathed a sigh of relief. She returned eagerly to her mission and the desk drawer. She felt around the secret compartment as far back as her hand could reach. Nothing! Then she pressed each side gently, to see if there was any give. As she was pushing the front, she felt it give ever so slightly, and so she pushed harder. Click! And the compartment opened, revealing a glowing green case. She gasped in excitement with this discovery. Eagerly, she grabbed the case, but jumped back as she felt the tingling in her arm. "Good grief, what is this thing anyway!" she exclaimed. "But the guys have been touching it, and they are still alive. Surely I can touch it too!" She quickly opened the case. The tingling in her hand went away.

Cheryl was disappointed to see only a pair of funky-looking glasses. "Well, dear brother," Cheryl said to herself, "You are really making a fashion statement. But they do glow nicely. Maybe you're coming up with a weird Halloween costume. I wonder what these look like when on?" She turned toward the mirror on the back of the door as she lifted the glasses to her eyes.

She stepped back in surprise and fear when she realized she was not alone. A smiling person dressed in a bodysuit was saying, "Don't worry about me. I'll do you no harm. I just wanted to compliment you for being such a clever one to discover these glasses. Your brother will be so upset."

Cheryl yanked the glasses off and looked around the room. She seemed to be alone. She shrugged her shoulders and lifted the glasses to her eyes once again.

Another person with a red heart on her forehead and wearing a golden bodysuit was pleading with her. "Oh, Cheryl, don't listen to him. You know it's not right to snoop in your brother's room and take his belongings without permission. You would hate it if someone did that to you."

Cheryl couldn't believe what she was seeing and hearing, so she removed the glasses again just to make sure where she really was. Larry's room looked just like she remembered it to be, and she and Tiger were alone. Or were they? Putting the glasses back to her eyes, she could see the other beings again. Plucking up her courage, she asked, "Who are you?"

"I'm C-tel, an angel from Good One's kingdom," spoke the being with the red heart. "I've been sent to protect you from harm and evil. Please put the glasses back."

The other being in a camouflage bodysuit stepped boldly forward, pushing C-tel out of the way. "And I'm here to help you make the *right* choice. After all this good detective work you have done, you should be honored with a reward. Keep the silly green case and see how your brother sweats! It may come in handy to bargain with him sometime in the future when you need a big favor from him. He may decide to tell on you for sneaking out at night. This could come in *very* handy."

Cheryl thought about it for a few seconds, and then made her decision.

Chapter 6

A New Friend

Larry heard a big crash behind him in the school hall. He turned to see a red-faced Jodi stooping to collect her books and belongings that were scattered on the floor in front of her.

"I'm such a klutz," Jodi murmured with a self-conscious giggle. "I tripped and caught myself, but not my load."

Larry began helping her gather her things. "I'm Larry Foster," he introduced himself. "You're new here this year, aren't you?"

"Yes," Jodi answered. "We moved here from Florida to be near Grandma and Grandpa."

"I see," Larry eased into conversation. "How do you like it here so far?" It was comfortable to talk to Jodi. Her brown eyes conveyed a sense of warmth and openness, and yet a bit of mystery that intrigued Larry. He liked her shy smile, which made him feel manly, as if he needed to protect her. And her freckled nose was just plain cute. They started walking toward homeroom.

"It's okay here. It just takes time to make friends again," she replied, a look of sadness in her eyes, "and . . ." Her voice faded away, and thinking better of what she was about to say, she changed the subject. "Well, I should probably glance at those spelling words one more time before the test. Why don't we talk some more another time?"

Larry nodded and walked to his desk beside Dave. "Are you scoring points?" Dave gave him that knowing smile.

"You're just jealous!" Larry retorted quickly, his face feeling a bit hot, "but you should meet her too. She's easy to talk to for a girl!"

When the students were dismissed to go to science class, Larry tried to make his way through the confusion to where Jodi was. Maybe they could talk some more. But when he got to her, he couldn't think of a thing to say. He felt so awkward, but fortunately, Jodi came to the rescue. "Hello, again!" she greeted him. "So have you gone to this school all your life?"

Larry nodded, and his nervousness disappeared. "I grew up here, just across town. I met my buddy, Dave, in third grade, and we've hung out ever since. So where do you live?"

"We live in the Cherrywood Apartments by the park," Jodi replied.

"Oh, I know where that is." Larry's voice rose with animation. "Dave and I go by there every time we ride our bikes in the park. We like to do the jumps there, and practice our stunts."

"Are you very good at it?" Jodi's eyes sparkled with interest.

"I don't know. We do have fun with it though."

"I'd like to watch you sometime," Jodi offered, thinking she'd like to get better acquainted with Larry. Being new to town and to school, she hadn't met many people her age yet. And Larry seemed friendly, his blue eyes smiled warmly, and he was not bad looking either. His sandy brown hair matched the shirt he was wearing. "I have Rollerblades and enjoy doing things in the park, too," she added.

"That sounds fun. If the weather is good this Sunday, why don't I drop by on the way to the park," Larry offered.

"Great!" Jodi responded. Her enthusiasm made Larry feel warm inside. He hoped Dave would not mind including another friend in their group. After all, how could one resist Jodi's smile and friendly ways? And she even liked to skate with her Rollerblades!

That afternoon after school, Larry hurried home. He was anxious to use ORB and talk to L-mor about being friends with Jodi. Entering his room, he sensed that something was different, and when his eyes rested on his desk, he gasped in amazement. The top desk drawer was gaping open. The secret compartment lay exposed, and there was nothing in it. ORB was gone!

He examined the secret compartment, and found it jammed. Who would have violated his privacy like this and stolen his possession? He looked around the room for clues.

"How are you feeling, dear?" Larry heard his mother's words coming from his sister's room.

Cheryl, of course! That conniving little sister of his must have discovered ORB. She played sick today so that she could snoop in his room. Anger welled up inside Larry, and he wanted to stomp right over to Cheryl's room and demand that she give ORB back. Common sense reminded him to cool down and think clearly about how to approach this ticklish event. Even though he could not see him, Larry sensed that L-mor was near, helping him keep calm. He must think what would be the next best thing to do. If he made too big a scene, the whole family would find out about ORB, and it would be even harder to keep ORB from being captured by the dark angels.

He must talk to Dave. Larry made a quick phone call, and they arranged to meet at the ball park where their Little League games were played. When Dave saw Larry's face, he could tell something was drastically wrong. "ORB is gone!" the words came spilling from Larry's mouth. "Cheryl played sick today and stayed home from school, and now the desk drawer is open, the compartment jammed open, and it's empty." Larry's fingers were clenched in a fist, and his movements were jerky in his nervousness. He continued, "I haven't accused Cheryl yet. I knew I'd make too big a scene, and Mom would get involved. I don't know what to do. Maybe if you come with me, you can help me talk to Cheryl."

It took a minute for Dave to grasp the impact of what Larry was telling him. "Sure," he said, "I'll help you. Maybe we can persuade her to give ORB back. Then we'll just have to include her in the secret, and tell her what ORB is all about."

Larry didn't like the idea of including his sister in their secret. He wasn't sure he could trust her. But at this point, their options were rather slim. At least, this way, they would get ORB back. He nodded in agreement, and they made their way to Larry's home.

They stood in the hallway in front of Cheryl's door, and took a deep breath. Larry knocked on the door. "It's your brother," he announced.

The door opened just a crack, and Cheryl spoke in a whisper, "What do you want?"

"We need to talk to you," Dave chimed in. Cheryl couldn't resist that, and the door opened.

Larry began, "Someone's been in my room today, jammed my desk drawer open, and taken something of mine. Since you were the only one home today, I thought you might know something about it."

"I don't know what you're talking about," Cheryl responded sweetly. "What are you missing?"

"A small green case," Larry answered.

"I haven't seen it," Cheryl lied.

"Ah, 'fess up. You know I could tell the folks about the other night." Larry stared at his sister intently. "Besides, who else was home today? It has to be you!"

"I don't have it!" Cheryl insisted. "Search for yourself. I give you permission to look around my room. I know it looks suspicious with me being home today and all. But I don't have it. Maybe someone climbed in through your window from the tree outside." She smiled at this clever thought.

"Right," Larry agreed sarcastically, "why didn't we think of that? We must talk to Tiger."

"Seriously," Dave interjected, "we would like to search your room. There is no other explanation we can think of."

"Whatever," Cheryl said as she sighed and rolled her eyes. The boys exchanged glances, and then began their search, in the closet, in drawers, in the knapsack, and under the bed. ORB was nowhere to be found. "See, I told you I don't have it," Cheryl responded self-righteously.

Chapter 7

The Private Investigators

The disappearance of ORB was a dilemma for boys. Dave polished his k-sun on his shirt. Without ORB, there was no way to know if he was making progress with his quest. If only they could talk to their golden angels, it would be so helpful. "I know they're with us," Dave said, "and trying to tell us what to do. But it's not the same. Let's really pay close attention to the thoughts we have. Maybe we'll hear what they're trying to tell us."

Larry nodded thoughtfully. "If Cheryl doesn't have ORB, then she's either hidden it very well or passed it on to a friend, like Winnie." Larry grimaced at that thought.

Dave spoke slowly, "If she's passed it on to a friend, it would most likely be a girl, and that's out of our league. We need to have a girl on our side. Do you think Jodi could be trusted?"

"I don't know, but she seems like she would," Larry replied eagerly. "I've asked her to come with us to the park on Sunday to watch us do some jumps with our bikes. She's bringing her Rollerblades. After we get to know her better and if we both feel comfortable with her, we can ask if she'd be interested in helping us."

Dave nodded in agreement, and then a hint of a smile played on his lips. "We can start our own spy ring! In the meantime, let's turn on all our antennas and keep our wits about us."

"For sure, Private Investigator!" Larry gave his friend a high five.

"Let's meet same time and place tomorrow to compare notes?" Dave suggested.

"Good plan," Larry agreed.

The next afternoon after school, the boys met to discuss their case. The baseball park where they often met was a grassy park where the neighborhood kids had batted many a ball. The boys had played with the Little League teams here. The park was conveniently located about halfway between Larry's and Dave's homes. Some oak trees bordered the open area, and there were a couple of park benches on one side. The boys were alone except for some squirrels busily gathering acorns. "Did you see Winnie today?" Larry asked. "She crowed like an old chicken and told me she knew something I didn't know."

"I bet Cheryl's given the ORB to her," Dave answered dejectedly. Together they plodded over the grass.

"That's what I think, too," Larry agreed. "It's my worst nightmare. On a more positive note, did you notice that I connected with Jodi again?"

"Yes," Dave responded with a smile. "I take it that you scored more points?"

Larry felt his face getting warm. "I'm just laying the groundwork in case we need a new partner," he replied. "And I'm feeling good about that."

Just then, Dave noticed a small glowing object at the foot of a tree the kids had named Open-Mouth. "Look," he said, pointing to the old tree with a black hole in its trunk. Its gnarled bark and the hole made the tree look like a person yawning. They stepped closer to the old tree to look at the object, and couldn't believe their eyes.

It was ORB, just lying on the ground. How lucky could they be? Eagerly Larry reached for the case and picked it up. But on opening the green case, he found it empty; the glasses had been removed. The boys searched carefully among the leaves that were on the ground, but without success. They peered into the mouth of the tree, but the glasses were not there.

"You know what I think?" Larry asked, putting his finger to the side of his head. "I think Cheryl put ORB in Open-Mouth as a pickup place for Winnie."

"I agree," Dave said. "So if Open-Mouth is being used by them, let's not spend too much time here and arouse suspicion."

"Good thinking. I'll see you later." Larry turned and headed for home.

When Sunday came, the weather was beautiful and sunny. Dave and Larry were ready for some time at the park. They found Jodi waiting outside her apartment, dressed in shorts and a T-shirt, her Rollerblades draped across her left shoulder. The boys pushed their bikes as the three walked toward the park.

When they got to the park, the boys insisted that Jodi use her Rollerblades. "Ladies first!" Larry said with a nod of the head. "The pavement is here, and our bike jumps are over there in the ravine." Besides, he thought, if they were going to include Jodi in their secret, the best place to tell her was where they had discovered ORB in the first place.

"Oh, all right," Jodi agreed, "but I feel self-conscious with you just watching. You need to ride with me." The boys nodded and propped their bikes against the bench and waited for her to get her gear on.

When she was ready, she smiled shyly, "This is the first time I've used these since coming to Warrenville. I hope I haven't forgotten how to blade!" But she glided easily over the pavement, as naturally as if she had skated every day. She started around the walk. "Come with me," she called.

The boys rode beside Jodi. "You're good on those wheels!" Larry exclaimed in admiration, as he watched her swaying rhythmically with even strides. Jodi beamed happily. After several rounds, they stopped to rest at a bench. "When did you learn to skate so well?" Larry panted.

A sad expression came over Jodi's face. "My folks used to fight a lot, and since I had Rollerblades and there was a park nearby, I did a lot of practicing just to get out of the house," she said. "I've used these skates a lot in the past two years before we came to Warrenville!"

"Sorry," Dave mumbled in sympathy. He thought about his own father, and how he also tried to escape his father's unpredictability.

"Now they've divorced," she continued, "and that's why my mom moved us to Warrenville to start a new life."

"Well, we're glad you're here," Larry encouraged. "Shall we do some more rounds, and then we'll go do some jumps?"

Jodi laughed and nodded. Picking up a small blue flag that someone had dropped on the ground, she called playfully, "See if you can get this away from me!"

The boys chased after her with their bikes. Just as Larry was about to catch the flag from her left hand, she changed it to her right. "I'll cover the right, and you the left!" Dave shouted instructions to his buddy. But Jodi was full of tricks, passing the flag back and forth between hands and legs. As the race continued around the walk, Jodi could not contain herself any longer and burst into giggles. At last Dave caught the flag and raced off in triumph. Larry was not to be outdone, and chased after his buddy, hoping to get the flag from him.

Jodi plopped on the bench to change into her street shoes. Before long, the boys were back, waving the poor little blue frayed flag. "Where do you jump your bikes?" Jodi asked.

"Come with us," Larry invited. As they headed toward the forested ravine, a small wind began to blow. "I'll check the trail to see if it's safe for you to come down," he told his buddy, remembering the rock that had been in the way last time. "And Jodi, can sit here to watch us jump," he added, pointing to a big log halfway down the hill and several feet from the path. "It's okay," Larry shouted up to Dave.

Soon Dave was whizzing past and flying off the jump and through the air. He landed perfectly, while Jodi clapped in glee. Next, Larry shot past, made his landing, and skidded to a stop. "You guys are good!" Jodi exclaimed.

After a few more jumps, the boys stopped at the bottom of the hill, and called Jodi to come. "We want to show you something," Larry said. He paused until she had joined them. "First of all, this has to be kept a secret, so you must promise not to tell a soul what we're about to tell you!"

Jodi's brown eyes grew serious. "I promise," she said.

Larry leaned against the tree and began in hushed tones, "A few weeks ago, right here under this tree, I found an unusual green case with the word ORB-6 engraved on the outside." He pulled the case from his pocket and showed it to Jodi. She carefully touched the glowing case and then drew her hand back quickly as she felt the tingling.

Dave laughed. "You should have seen Larry jump the first time he touched this case. He kicked it over there in the woods, and I had to go find it!"

Larry ignored Dave's teasing. "The tingling goes away soon. Inside this case, was a pair of funny-looking glasses. We called them ORB for short. When we tried them on, we were able to see and talk to golden beings from another planet. They called themselves angels from Good One's kingdom. They explained that they were giving us the glasses so we could see how they help us. You probably think we're crazy!"

"I . . . I . . . I don't know what to think," Jodi stammered. "So where are the glasses?"

"They got stolen," Larry said. "The angels have some enemies that wear camouflage bodysuits and use dart guns. We were told that they hate the special glasses. The good angels warned us that the enemy would try to get rid of the glasses. So we believe they are responsible for the glasses disappearing. I kept them in my room, and they disappeared the day my sister played sick and stayed home. We also think Winnie knows something about the glasses because she's been giving us smart remarks when she sees us." Larry paused to see if Jodi was still with him or ready to run away.

"These glasses were so cool," Dave chimed in. "We saw some amazing things when we used them. We could replay things that happened to us, and see how the angels persuaded us and others to make the choices we do. When I had trouble at home, I could see how the good and evil angels were influencing my dad and me."

"Yeah," Larry agreed. "I saw how the enemy angels helped Winnie get me in trouble at school. I had to go talk to the school principal."

Jodi pondered, "I wonder if I would be able to see why my parents got divorced."

"I think so," Dave replied. "ORB worked for me. It helped to be able to talk to the good angels about the hard things that happen."

Larry stepped back from the tree and continued, "We don't expect you to believe everything we're telling you 'til you see for yourself. But we would like your help to find the missing glasses. Will you help us crack this case, and recover the glasses?"

Just then a gust of wind blasted through the ravine, and a large dead branch fell a few inches from Larry. "Wow!" Dave exclaimed. "I bet if we had ORB, we'd see how that branch really fell!"

They looked around suspiciously, knowing they were not alone, but without ORB they could see no one. "I know L-mor is here," Larry said with conviction. "He had to be the one who told me to move back from the tree so I'd be safe! Thanks, L-mor!"

Just then, a small silver piece plunked on the ground by Larry's feet. "It's another piece for my k-sun! See, L-mor is here!" Excitedly, he fit the piece on his k-sun and snapped it in place. Dave and Jodi stepped forward to admire the k-sun.

"Cool," Dave grinned.

Looking above to see if there were any more dead branches, Larry resumed his conversation with Jodi. "So can you help us find ORB?"

Jodi looked at the fallen branch, at Larry's k-sun, and then at the boys' faces. She nodded thoughtfully and asked, "What would you like me to do?"

"We'd like you to keep an eye on Cheryl and Winnie," Dave said, "and see if you can learn anything about the glasses. Do you know who they are?"

"I found out who Winnie was when she about ran over me one day going to class," Jodi responded, "but I haven't met Cheryl."

"Sounds like Winnie all right. Cheryl is my sister," Larry said. "She's in the eighth grade. I'll bring you a picture of her."

"It might work better," Dave cautioned Jodi, "if they don't know you are in on our secret, or that you are included in the recovery mission."

"Right," Jodi agreed. "Got-ya! How will I let you know if I've learned something about the glasses?"

"Good thought," Dave pondered. "What if we signal each other with something green, you know, like a green light?"

"I like that," Larry agreed. "I have a green notebook that I'll point to when you're looking."

Jodi giggled with delight. "I'll put a green string on my backpack, and will rub it when I need to talk to you."

"Where is the best place to meet?" Larry asked. "Is the ball park after school okay?" The others thought for a few seconds and then nodded in agreement.

Before leaving for home, the youths pledged their desire to be a team by joining hands, raising them toward the sky, and then dashing them downward with a "yes" shout. It was their way to express a solemn pact for their mission.

Chapter 8

Unlocking the Mystery

The day after the PI (Private Investigators) team began their work was uneventful, except that Larry's sister Cheryl came to him and apologized for lying to him. She confessed that she had taken ORB and had hidden it in Open-Mouth tree. She had then phoned Winnie of the hiding place, just as the PI team had suspected. Winnie treated Cheryl rudely as soon as she'd gotten ORB. There was no thank-you to Cheryl. And when she discovered what was in the green ORB case, she fussed and fumed. "What's so special about an old pair of glasses!" she had said. Cheryl then realized what a mistake she had made in helping Winnie. She regretted her actions.

"How can I make it up to you?" Cheryl asked Larry. She seemed to be sincere.

"Help us get the glasses back," Larry responded, stooping down to pet Tiger, who was rubbing his leg. "Do you know where she put them?"

"No, I don't," Cheryl answered apologetically. "She just made a smart remark when I asked her about the glasses today. She's gotten what she wants from me, and so now I'm dirt."

"Well," Larry said, "if you find out anything, let me know." He thought about telling her about their PI team, but then discarded that idea. He still wasn't sure how far Cheryl could be trusted.

Tuesday morning in homeroom, Larry looked across the room to Jodi. Her eyes were sparkling with excitement. She was still holding her backpack and methodically stroking the green string she had attached to the zipper pull.

Larry nodded in acknowledgment of the signal. "Jodi's got a clue!" he whispered to Dave. "We meet at the park after school."

The PI team could hardly wait for school to end, as their excitement mounted. When Larry and Dave wheeled into the park on their bikes, they saw Jodi waiting on a bench, her Rollerblades slung over her shoulder.

"What is it?" the boys chorused simultaneously.

"I think Winnie has the glasses in her locker," Jodi began. "They fell out on the floor as I just happened to be walking by this morning, and she scooped them up in a big hurry and tossed them in the bottom of the locker. Her locker number is 66."

"Her locker!" Larry cried in exasperation. "Man, how will we get into her locker?"

"Shall we go to the school now, see if it's open?" suggested Dave. "My father has been telling me how to figure out lock combinations. I can try to figure it out."

"Do you think we should?" Jodi asked with some caution.

Larry hesitated, but then remembering that L-mor would be with him, his hesitation left him. He picked up his bike. "Let's go. The janitor might still be there, and ORB is pretty important. Do you know how to ride double?" he asked Jodi.

"I think so," Jodi laughed as she wriggled onto the bicycle bar in front of Larry's seat. Jodi became quiet as they rode to the school. She was feeling a sense of safety being so close to Larry's body as they rode along with his arms almost enveloping her. She had not felt this way since she was a little girl, and her mother had scooped her into her lap to comfort her when she was hurt or upset. It had been a long time since that had happened. Her mother seemed to be wearing a coat of iron armor ever since her problems with her dad and the divorce. It hid all the warmth and love that once was part of her nature. Jodi was the one who suffered from that, and this bike ride with Larry stirred feelings deep within her.

The school was very quiet when they rode up. The front doors were locked, and there were no cars outside. "Let's try the door on the end," Dave suggested. There were big smiles all around when that door opened. They noticed a car parked nearby. "That must be the janitor's car," Dave remarked.

They felt very awkward as they tiptoed down the silent hallway, talking in whispers. "We need to cover for Dave, and let him know if anyone is coming," said Larry, watching over his shoulder. "Jodi, you watch the front door, and I'll watch the back. Whistle a tune to signal if anyone's coming!"

Jodi chuckled to herself as she thought about what tune would be the best, just in case.

Dave found the locker, and then worked and worked on the lock. He tried different combinations in response to the little clicks he heard. Nothing seemed to work. The seconds and minutes ticked by. Larry and Jodi, as guards, were tense, becoming more and more nervous with the thought of getting caught. Dave found himself feeling flustered with the lock that would not respond to the turns and twists he tried.

Just then, Jodi heard footsteps, and she began to whistle a strangely familiar tune. Dave heard the signal and scurried to the end of the hall. Larry held the door open for them as an escape. They heard footsteps in the distance as the door closed behind them. There was silence as they waited and waited. What had happened to Jodi?

At last the door opened, and there was the janitor with a large garbage can full of trash. They were all surprised to see each other. "What are you boys doing here?" he asked suspiciously.

"I, I forgot something in my locker." It was the best lie Dave could come up with, even though his body language did not convey such an innocent mission.

The janitor was a big burly man with broad shoulders and muscular arms that bulged from the sleeves of a well-worn T-shirt. But underneath the bushy eyebrows were kindly eyes. He pondered the situation a second and decided to give the boys a break. "Well, you're pretty lucky I'm still here and the door is open. Hurry up now, I give you five minutes to get in and out!"

The boys darted down the hall. "Jodi, Jodi, where are you? Come quick!" Larry spoke, his voice sounding hollow as it echoed back from the bare walls.

Just then, Jodi stepped into the hall from the girls' restroom. Larry and Dave grabbed her hands and rushed to the door. "The janitor knows we're here, but not you," Larry warned. "Don't let him see you or we're in big trouble! He went that way!" The boys pointed to the back of the school where the dumpsters were.

Jodi slipped around the opposite corner while the boys picked up their bikes. They disappeared around the corner just as the janitor was returning.

"That was close," Larry whispered to Jodi, as he steadied the bike for her to get on.

"Yes," Jodi responded. "And I have something exciting to tell you when it's safe!"

The boys exchanged eye contact but rode in silence back to the park. Jodi was whistling the familiar tune, and then a smile would break out on her face spontaneously. "Do you know what I found?" Jodi began when they reached the park bench. She reached in her pocket and pulled out ORB. The lenses were cracked, and the frames were bent. "Is this what you are looking for?" she asked.

Dave and Larry gasped and looked around to make sure they were alone. "Where did you find these?" Dave blurted out.

"In the girls' restroom—in the garbage!" Jodi glowed triumphantly. "I dashed in there to hide when I heard the janitor. Winnie must have thrown them away just before she left school today. The scary thing is the janitor came to get the garbage can while I was in there, and I had to hide in one of the toilet stalls. My heart was pounding so loud I was sure he was going to hear me!"

Larry and Dave chuckled at Jodi's story and shook their heads in disbelief. It was nothing short of a miracle that ORB had been found just minutes before the janitor had emptied the garbage can with these special glasses in it.

Larry gently touched ORB's cracked lenses. They looked so misshapen and forlorn. "I wonder if they still work," he said sadly. He gently bent the frames back into a more normal shape.

"Let's take a look," Dave suggested. "There's no one around."

Chapter 9

The Sinister Summit

Larry gently put ORB to his eyes. They no longer fit to his face because they were so twisted, but as he held the cracked lenses to his eyes, Larry could still make out the figures of the angels, though not as clearly. It was good to see the smiling face of his special angel, L-mor, and feel the pat on the back that he gave. "It's good to see you again," he joked, putting words in Larry's mouth.

Larry smiled and said, "It's good to *see* you too!" He then shared the glasses with Dave, and then with Jodi.

It was Jodi's first experience with ORB, and despite the poor images through the cracked lenses, she was still amazed at the scene before her. A golden angel with a heart on her forehead stepped forward and touched Jodi. "I'm J-gette (pronounced Jay-get), the angel assigned to help and protect you," she smiled. "I'm with you as long as you want me!"

"Oh, thank you," Jodi murmured.

"I know you have been talking to your new friends, so you've learned a bit about us angels. I also have a little gift for you," J-gette held out a little knobby wire heart attached to a chain. The framework created hints of cracks in the heart. "It's called a k-sun. It stands for your quest to find love and acceptance. I know that is the desire of your heart. As you journey with Good One's team, you will find the happiness you seek. Each time you reach a milestone, you will receive a special piece that will fit on these knobs. Treasure it with all your heart."

"Thank you, I will," Jodi responded as she rubbed the k-sun between her fingers and thumb. Then Jodi glanced down and noticed dark strands entwining her legs so that it was hard to walk freely. A short distance away was an evil angel with a spool of dark weblike strands. He darted this way and that behind J-gette, waiting for a chance to wrap some more strands about Jodi.

"What are these?" Jodi asked her special angel, pointing to the strands wrapped around her legs.

J-gette explained, "The angel from the legion of devaluation is trying to capture you for Hesperus's kingdom. The evil angel starts weaving his web slowly at first so that you don't notice what's happening."

"Oh, but I don't want to be part of Hesperus's kingdom!" Jodi cried. "Can you get me untangled?"

"I would be thrilled to do that for you. Your word is my command!" J-gette eagerly touched the dark threads, and they evaporated into a swarm of little bugs as small as fleas. The bugs took flight and swarmed to the evil angel like a magnet. The angel did not look pleased as the little bugs landed on his head and disappeared into his hair. He scratched and scratched his head in discomfort, and plopped down on a nearby rock and pouted.

And then Jodi saw something so amazing and fearful, she could say nothing but watch. Her face froze in a concentrated effort to comprehend what she was seeing through the cracked lenses of ORB. Before her, a giant gray enclosure came silently out of the ground. It was shaped like a huge wasp's nest, constructed with billions of strands of threads, similar to the few that had been wrapped around her legs. Then hundreds and hundreds of the angels in camouflage suits appeared in a dizzying display of speed, leaving streaks of black that led to a large opening in the side of the hive. All the angels had a colored arrowhead on their chests, some blue, others yellow, red, and all the colors in between.

"What's happening?" Jodi finally gathered courage to ask.

Jodi's angel explained, "Hesperus is having a planning session. It's a dreadful thing to witness. But it might be helpful for you to know more about the enemy we fight. I'll call for some help to keep us safe, and you can go peek inside the Capture Cave." J-gette touched the heart on her forehead, and immediately there were a dozen golden angels surrounding them. "Move into position," J-gette instructed Jodi.

Jodi moved slowly forward, holding ORB in place. "Hey," shouted an evil voice. "We don't want no earthworms around here. Get out of here!" Jodi trembled with fright. The thought of being called an "earthworm" made her shudder.

"We'll keep you safe," encouraged J-gette, handing her a cream-colored cloak. "Put this on and snap it shut. It will make you invisible. Then continue moving into position."

Jodi could see the golden angels defending her as a crowd of evil angels began to gather. "Hey, where did she go? We know she's in there somewhere!" they shouted as they surrounded the group of golden angels. They tried again and again to strike blows or pull a golden angel from its protective position, but without success.

At last Jodi was in position to see inside the cave. And because things were happening inside, the evil angels gave up their struggle with the angels protecting Jodi. Inside the cave, there were lots of evil angels listening to a tall speaker. It seemed as if a dark cloud hovered over them all. In front of the gathering was a screen with a picture of a human who was completely wrapped up in the dark threads, forming a black cocoon around him. Sinister laughing rippled across the audience.

The tall speaker in front said, "I'd like to call Leo from the Revenge Legion to the front to receive the award for his team. They've done a good job, and this sucker pictured here is just one of many this team has captured for our cause. We won't have any more trouble from this one, and from now on, he'll work for us!" A big cheer arose from the audience.

"Now," the speaker said, "I'd like to have a report from the various leaders of the legions. Listen up, gang, so we can all work together." One by one, the evil angels with the arrowheads on their chests came forward. They looked sinister as they displayed pictures on the screen of their victims and projects. There was wicked laughter, as they discussed plans to overcome the earthlings. And if one legion was having less success than others, reinforcements were assigned to join them.

The speaker announced another group. "We'd like a report from the commander of the Acts of God Army." A fierce-looking angel stepped forward. "We have had a lot of success with the earthquakes and hurricanes lately," he said as cheers arose from the group. Movies of the evil army were shown on the screen. The scenes looked like huge riots taking place in the middle of the earthquake or hurricane, with the evil angels toppling buildings and bridges, and breaking dams. They were bent on anything that would crush or kill people. "The marvelous thing about our work," said the commander, "is that God gets the blame for all the chaos we create. People often call natural disasters 'Acts of God.' Silly critters. If only they knew!" Laughter roared across the room.

At this, Jodi turned to her golden angel and asked, "What are they talking about?"

"God is another name for Good One," J-gette replied. "They're laughing because Good One is getting blamed for the bad things that happen."

"I see," Jodi replied, and then turned back to watch the summit.

When the army commander had finished, the tall speaker arose. "Let me remind you of the overall plan we have which has proven very successful." A thundering "yes" arose from the audience. The speaker raised his hand and continued, "First, we want humans to think they are Number One, the ultimate, that they are always right, and that they should get whatever their little heart's desire to make them successful and beautiful. Second, of course, *we* know that *they* are not Number One, so when they are disappointed, throw discouragement, revenge, fear, and addictions their way! Third, destroy the infrastructure by polluting the environment, causing natural disasters, infecting the media and TV with our agenda, and creating comfort food and medicines that will cause sickness and death to humans. Study your little earthworms. Whatever numbs their minds so that they can't think clearly will be to our advantage. They become as weak as water in our hands!" Wicked chuckles came from the audience, which moved the speaker to grin widely, obviously pleased with himself.

Again the speaker raised his hands for silence. "That's our offense plan, gang. You remember what our defense plan is?"

"Obliterate all ORBs," the audience cried.

"Yes, and . . ." the speaker prompted.

"Undermine the Oracles," the audience chorused again.

"Exactly," the speaker confirmed. "Go, and do your worst!"

At this, the huge Capture Cave began to descend into the ground again. With the sinister summit dismissed, some of the evil angels again turned their attention to the band of golden angels surrounding Jodi. But the golden angels defended themselves and gradually worked their way to the edge of the field. At last, the evil angels gave up their struggle and left with scowls on their faces. J-gette unsnapped the special cloak that had kept Jodi invisible and tucked it under one arm. "That was a sobering scene," J-gette said, giving Jodi a comforting hug. "And now you've had a look at Hesperus, the tall angel who led out in the summit. He's the one who started the war in the beginning."

Jodi felt overwhelmed with all the events she had just witnessed. Her arms felt stiff from clutching ORB so tightly. Slowly she lowered ORB from her eyes and flexed her arms. Larry and Dave approached her, with questions in their eyes. "Help me back to the bench," she said weakly, giving ORB carefully back to Larry. "I'll tell you what I saw."

As Jodi recounted all that she had seen and heard, Larry and Dave were astonished. "That's amazing," Dave commented. "It's hard to believe."

"I know," Larry agreed. The young people talked for a long time about Good One, Guerdon, Zephyr, their team of angels, and the war between good and evil.

"I want to make sure I am *not* on Hesperus's side," Dave said with determination.

"I want to be *on* the Good One's side," Jodi's voice was strong with conviction. Everyone nodded in agreement.

"Let's make a pact to join Good One's team," Larry suggested.

"Yes, yes," Dave and Jodi chorused, moving forward. One by one, they stacked their hands on top of each other's. "What shall we say?"

"Repeat after me," Larry volunteered. "I do solemnly swear . . . to join the Good One's team . . . to defend his ways . . . and put down evil . . . so help us, God." Dave and Jodi spoke the words with determination. The three young people moved their joined hands in unison up and down three times to confirm their decision. "Go, Good One," said Jodi with feeling.

"Yes, yes," Larry and Dave chorused as they each raised a fist in the air.

"There's something else," Jodi said. "I wonder what the Oracles are that they were talking about. We know what ORB is, but what did they mean by 'undermine the Oracles'?"

Before they could answer, Jodi glanced at her watch. "Oh, oh!" she exclaimed. "I've got to go. I've got an appointment with my mom in five minutes."

"We'll see you tomorrow. Our PI team can continue its quest for the Oracles then," Larry called as her slim figure hurried toward home.

Chapter 10

Discovering the Oracles

When Larry got home, Tiger came running to greet him. His fur was all fluffed out, his tail like a bottle brush. "What have you been up to?" Larry reached down to pet his cat, as a soft whimper came from the neighbor's front steps. "Oh," Larry understood immediately. "You've been chasing off the neighbor's dog, have you? Good cat! You protect us from all those dangerous creatures." Larry smiled at the neighbor's little dog who was trembling, blinking his eyes, and licking his lips nervously. "What a brave cat!" Larry chuckled, talking to Tiger as he opened the door.

When he was safely in his room, Larry carefully removed ORB from his pocket. Sadly he touched the bent frame and cracked lenses and wished that they could be fixed. Winnie had really thrashed them, but at least they were back in his possession. Sometime, he'd have to ask L-mor if they could be fixed. In the meantime, he felt an urgency to understand what was meant by the word Oracles, but he wanted to do that with his friends. So he gently placed ORB in its case and put it in the special pocket in his backpack for tomorrow.

There was a gentle tap on his door. His mom opened it. "Don't forget you have a dental appointment at 4:00 p.m. after school tomorrow. Do you need me to come be with you?" Mrs. Foster asked.

"I don't think so," Larry replied. "It's just a checkup, right?" His mother nodded.

"So you'll ride your bike to school tomorrow for transportation?"

Larry nodded, but his mind was twirling. How would his PI team find time to understand what the Oracles were? If they couldn't meet after school, then maybe they could get together at the lunch hour break. But where could they meet where they could be alone and not discovered? Then he thought of the library building. The second floor had the big thick reference books, with high shelves and few people. Maybe that would work.

The three friends gathered at noon and entered the library, one by one making their way to the second floor. They found a small table and chair at the end of one of the stacks, and luckily they were alone. In silence they gathered about Larry as he pulled ORB's case from his backpack. Carefully, he lifted the glasses to his eyes. He smiled as he greeted L-mor. "We are curious to know what the Oracles are that the evil angels are trying to undermine."

L-mor's countenance brightened, and he smiled as he explained: "It is the ancient record of the Good One's history with the people of this world. It was written by faithful followers. It even tells of our commander, Guerdon's wonderful mission to earth. Down through the ages, Hesperus and his angels have tried to destroy the Oracles, because it explains about the war between good and evil. At one point, he was almost successful in destroying it, but we have been protecting it since its beginnings. It is now printed in such abundance, that almost every home in this country has one. They've called it the Holy Bible, and there are several copies in this building. See the lights down there?" He pointed down the aisle, and a soft light was enveloping some books.

Larry made his way down the aisle, and looked up at the glowing books. Carefully, he removed one from the shelf and showed it to his friends. The book seemed old, so he opened it carefully. The fragile pages were yellowed, and it smelled of mildew. He wondered why he had not heard more about the Holy Bible if it had been around for a long time.

L-mor continued, "Since the Oracles are now so plentiful in various versions, the evil angels just try to keep people from seeing it, wanting it, reading it, or understanding it. But it is so important, as it is the guiding light for earthlings to know about the Good One and his kingdom. It's another tool the Good One has provided so our *kananas* are able to find and choose the right way to Good One."

"Interesting," Larry commented, as he slowly turned the pages. "Do we have these in our homes?"

"Yes," L-mor replied eagerly, "but I'm afraid you'll have to hunt for them. They are rarely used."

Just then, the sound of steps on the stairs brought the youths back to their three-dimensional world. Larry quickly handed the book to Dave while he slipped ORB into his pocket.

The librarian was a gray-haired lady with outdated clothes, and a white undergarment showing underneath the hem of her dress. She had a sour look on her face. "Are you finding everything you want?" she asked, as if forcing herself to be polite.

"I think so," Dave said. "We were just looking at this copy of the Holy Bible."

The librarian frowned and said accusingly, "Isn't that a bit boring for someone of your age? The children's books are downstairs. I think you should come down, now." It was clear that she did not trust them without adult supervision. Larry wondered if she knew how important the Oracles were, or if she had ever seen the light that glowed around them.

"We'll get our things and come down now," Larry responded politely. He noticed that when not looking through ORB's lenses, the Holy Bible looked just the same as any other book on the shelf. The fifth dimension glow had disappeared.

As the friends were leaving the library, they decided they would try to find a copy of the Oracles at their homes that evening. They were curious how a book of ancient times could be considered such a weapon in the universal struggle between good and evil.

* * *

Jodi was the first one home from school. She let herself into the apartment. She did not expect her mother to get home from work until after 6:00 p.m. This would give her time to hunt for the Oracles. She put her backpack in her room, grabbed an apple from the fruit bowl, and then began looking through the books in the bookcase. One by one she read the titles, but there was no Holy Bible there. She opened the door to her mother's room. She rarely went here, perhaps out of habit from the time when her father lived with them. As she scanned the room, her eyes rested on the nightstand by her mother's bed. There was a book, but when looking at it more closely, it was not the Bible. She decided she'd ask her mother when she got home. In the meantime, she'd work on her homework.

* * *

When Dave got home, he was thinking of the Oracles as well, but he wondered if his dad was away so that it would be safe to search the house. Finding everything quiet, he knew his first job was to do his chores. The consequences would not be pleasant if his dad should return and find them not done. But as Dave cleared the table of dirty dishes, he thumbed through the pile of newspapers and magazines at the end of the table. There were no books in the stack.

After the dishes were clean and put away, Dave moved into the small living room. He opened the shabby blinds and looked around the room. On the end table beside his dad's recliner were empty bottles and cans, and two full ashtrays. He disgustedly removed the litter and tidied up his dad's corner. How he wished his dad would do something in the evenings besides drink, smoke, and watch TV. Other fathers went with their kids to ball games or on camping trips. But there was no use thinking about that right now. Where would the Oracles be in his house?

Against one wall, the TV nestled in the middle of a network of shelves supported by black frames. Through the years, the shelves had accumulated various things. Among them stood his Little League trophy, and a knickknack with a snow scene encased in glass. He turned the miniature scene upside down and watched the snowflakes settle upon the little village inside the glass ball. Then he looked at the picture of his mother, who had died when he was five years old. He could hardly remember her now, but he gazed at her picture frequently to keep her memory etched in his mind. Another shelf had a disheveled row of books of assorted sizes, probably his mother's, as he had never seen his dad read a book. One by one he examined the books, looking for the Bible, but without success.

Then his eyes turned to the old coffee table in front of the sagging brown couch. The table was covered with newspapers. Dave thumbed through the untidy piles of papers, to see if there was anything else hidden among the pages. There was a bottom shelf to the coffee table, and it, too, was full. There were stacks of old magazines, most of them back copies of *Sports Illustrated.* But at one end, and on the very bottom of the stack of magazines, was a big book. Dave pulled it out and blew the dust from its edges. As he wiped his sleeve across the front, he could see a gold design that framed a small picture painted by an old master artist. The gold lettering was in fancy font, but Dave made out the words, "Holy Bible." How exciting. He had found the Oracles!

Afraid of being caught with something that his father would not approve of, he quickly put the magazines back as he had found them, and hurriedly carried the big book to his bedroom for safekeeping. He grabbed an old towel from the bathroom to use as a cover to disguise his treasure in case his dad arrived unexpectedly. Dave sat on the edge of his bed and opened the front cover. There were the words, "Given to David Lister and Mary Warren on their wedding day, June 4, 1988, from Mom and Dad Warren." This was his parents' wedding gift from his grandparents. What a discovery! He turned the page and found recorded the names and birthdates for his grandparents, his parents, and then his name and birth date. This must have been his mother's handwriting. A feeling of awe came over him, as if he had discovered a part of who he was.

Just then he heard the front door opening. He tucked the towel around the book and quickly slipped it under his bed. His father's angry voice shattered the excitement of the moment. "Couldn't you see the leaves need raking?" Dave's father fumed. "What have you been doing all afternoon, you useless son?"

* * *

After Larry's dental appointment, he pedaled his bike home with purpose. He wanted to see if he could find a copy of the Oracles at his house. The dry leaves along the street swirled up behind him, but he hardly noticed them. And Tiger only received a quick pat on the head for a greeting as Larry bounded up the stairs two at a time. "Anybody home?" he called as he slipped his backpack off and tossed it in his room.

A muffled voice came from behind Cheryl's door. That would be workable. Larry knew that he could safely search the rest of the house if Cheryl was occupied with something in her room. He returned downstairs to look through the bookshelves. The Fosters had plenty of books, and Larry started looking methodically from shelf to shelf. There was the set of *Encyclopedia Britannica* and the *Child Craft* set. There were *Reader's Digest* condensed books, biographies, classics, children's stories, gardening books, and on and on. Suddenly Larry was aware that there were footsteps on the stairs. Cheryl was coming. What should he do?

"What-cha doing?" Cheryl asked as she sauntered into the room with a curious look in her eyes.

"I'm looking for a certain book," Larry replied, as he continued to focus on the shelves.

"Hmm," Cheryl responded, apparently satisfied with his answer. "I think I'll have a soda." She turned toward the kitchen, got her drink, and then on to the family room. Larry could hear the TV going now.

When Larry had gone through all the bookshelves, he was disappointed that he had not found anything with the word Bible in the title. But there were some more books in the family room, and then some in the office. Perhaps he'd check the office first, before his folks got home. But that, too, was unsuccessful. He paused at the door to the family room, wondering if he should look there. He decided that it wouldn't hurt his cause if Cheryl found out what he was looking for. Maybe she would even help him. So he walked to the bookshelves and began his search there.

"Still haven't found it?" Cheryl questioned. "What's the title?"

"It's called Holy Bible," Larry responded.

"I don't remember anything like that. We must not have it," Cheryl replied.

Larry was disappointed, and then he had an idea. Why hadn't he thought of it before? ORB could help him! But he would have to be careful. He bounded up the stairs to his room and removed ORB carefully from its case. Perhaps it would be safe to check his parents' bedroom.

Quietly he stepped into the hall and listened to make sure Cheryl was still watching TV. Tiptoeing down the hall, he found the bedroom door slightly ajar. It squeaked as he opened it, but looking over his shoulder, it still seemed safe to proceed. The curtains were drawn, and the room was dim. Turning on the light, he looked around. The dresser was on one wall, a chest on the other, and closets spanned the third wall. But a king-size bed was against the fourth wall, and on either side of it were nightstands with various collections of reading materials—mostly books and magazines.

Putting ORB carefully to his eyes, he scanned the books on the nightstands, hoping for a glimpse of that soft glow he had seen at the library earlier that day. There was nothing, but he noticed L-mor nearby, a smile on his face. "You're getting warmer," he said. Larry smiled back, remembering the times his mother had helped him search for Easter eggs or some other item, using the "hot" or "cold" hints. Larry moved to a nightstand and opened the doors that opened into the compartment underneath. A soft glow from one of the books met his gaze. Carefully removing it, he read the title, "The New Jerusalem Bible."

"Congratulations, you have found a version of the Holy Bible," L-mor explained. "This version contains additional ancient writings to what is included in other Bible publications, but all Bibles tell the stories of our *kananas* as they have wrestled with the forces of good and evil."

Larry opened the book. "In the beginning, God created heaven and earth . . ." he read. He wanted to read more, but then realized that he was in his parents' room, uninvited, and began to feel like an intruder. Perhaps he should put the book back and ask permission to borrow it later.

Hearing his mother's voice downstairs, he realized she was home. Larry quickly replaced the book and closed the nightstand. He stopped in his room to replace ORB in its green case and then bounded down the stairs to greet his mother.

"How was your dental appointment?" Mrs. Foster asked with her motherly concern.

"No new cavities," grinned Larry. "Can I help you with supper?"

"Sure," she responded. "You can set the table."

As Larry started for the dish cupboard, he decided to launch his request. "Mom, I've been searching for something today. I'm looking for a Holy Bible. I looked in all the bookcases downstairs, and when I had no luck, I got real snoopy and looked in the nightstands in your bedroom. I hope you don't mind, but I found a New Jerusalem Bible there, and wondered if I could borrow it."

Mrs. Foster looked puzzled at first, and then smiled as she recalled the book. "Sure, you can have it if you want. I bid on a box of books at an auction a few years ago, and that book was included in the box. I have no interest in it. Help yourself."

"Thanks, Mom," responded Larry.

"You are weird, brother!" Cheryl volunteered in her usual sisterly manner.

"Thanks to you, too, dear sister," Larry quipped back. "I appreciate the compliment!"

Just then, there was urgent banging on the back door. "Don't knock the door down," Larry called as he opened the door.

There was Dave, with tears in his eyes.

Chapter 11

Camping at Paradise

"I need help," Dave's voice was trembling as he tried to hold back the tears. "Do you have a rake I can borrow? My dad is *really* mad at me for not raking the leaves in our yard, and I can't find our rake. I'm scared what he's going to do to me."

"Sure, just a minute," was Larry's quick response. "Mom, I'll be late for supper. Dave needs help."

Mrs. Foster took it all in and understood immediately. "No problem."

Larry quickly ran to the tool shed, found two leaf rakes, and grabbed the box of leaf bags. "Let's hustle. We'll have the job done in no time at all."

Dave gave him a relieved look. He remembered the saying from somewhere, "There's safety in numbers." He knew his dad would go easy on him if Larry were there.

* * *

After school the next day, Larry was anxious to meet with the PI team to see how successful his friends had been at finding their own copy of the ancient Oracles. With their signal system, they arranged to meet at the park after school. The autumn sun was still peeking through the few leaves left on the tree branches. More leaves lay as a crunchy blanket beneath the trees. Jodi was waiting for the boys as they rolled up on their bikes. She smiled in greeting, and giggled as Larry balanced the bike on the back tire. "Guess what I found under my pillow this morning?" Jodi's eyes sparkled as she held up her k-sun with another silver piece on it. "I don't know why it was there. I'm anxious to talk to J-gette and find out more."

"I should have brought ORB with me," Larry sighed. "Did you find a copy of the Oracles in your home?"

Jodi told about her unsuccessful search in her apartment. "But," she went on, "I talked to my mom when she got home, and she said she would get me a Gideon Bible from her workplace. They are given out free there. I hope she'll bring it home from work today with her."

Larry shared the story of his search and success, and then how his mother had given him a copy for his very own. Dave and Jodi clapped at his news and gave their friend a high five. They shifted their gaze to Dave, waiting to hear his story.

"I found a wonderful treasure," Dave began as he told his friends about finding the family Bible his grandparents had given his parents. "I have never known my grandparents. My father got very upset with me one time when I asked about them. I didn't even know their names!"

"Are they still alive?" Jodi wondered. "Wouldn't it be cool if you could find them? I love my grandparents."

Dave's voice betrayed his emotion, "It would be the best thing that ever happened to me."

Larry was excited for Dave too. "When we're through here, let's go to my place and Google their names on my computer," he offered, "and see what we can find." Dave seemed pleased.

Jodi was quiet with mixed emotions as she pondered going to Larry's home. She changed the subject. "Did you guys have time to read anything in your Bibles?"

"Not much," Larry said. "I read that God created the world in the beginning, and then scanned through a bunch of history stuff from a long time ago."

"I read a little last night after I heard my dad snoring," Dave offered. "The last book has a bunch of dreams that a man from the olden days had, and the last dream he had was of victory of the heavenly king and a description of the home he wants for us humans to live in. It sounded too good to be true—no hunger, no sickness, no one being hurt . . ." Dave's voice was filled with longing as he thought of how many times his father had hurt him.

"Wow," Larry said. "That fits in with what our angels have been telling us. I need to ask L-mor more about what to read. It seems like a complicated book. I wasn't sure about that first part. It sounded like Greek mythology or something. It said that the Good One (or God as it calls him in the Bible) made our world in six days! I've never heard anything like that in science class."

The friends were quiet for a moment as they thought about their new discoveries. Larry broke the silence. "Do you want to come over to my house now? Jodi, would you feel comfortable meeting my sister and my family? I've been hoping my sister would find better friends to hang out with. Winnie just gets her into trouble. I can show you the copy of my Bible, and Dave and I can search on the computer for his grandparents . . ." Larry made eye contact with his friends to see how they were responding to his suggestion.

"I think that would be okay," Jodi answered cautiously. "My mom doesn't get home from work until after six."

"I'll get you home before then," Larry promised. "Are you brave enough to ride with me on my bike again?"

Jodi felt her cheeks getting warm, but she nodded and hoped she didn't look too eager as she balanced herself on Larry's bike.

Larry's mom and sister, Cheryl, were in the kitchen/family room when the three friends arrived. Larry introduced Jodi, and then explained how the three of them had been trying to find a copy of the Bible to read.

"Oh yes," Mrs. Foster said. "Why don't you show Jodi the copy you found last night?"

"I will," Larry headed for the stairs. "I'll be right back."

When Larry returned with the Bible, Jodi and Cheryl seemed to be chatting comfortably. "I'll leave this for you and Cheryl to look at, Jodi, while Dave and I go up to my room to do that Google search."

"Sure," Jodi agreed, feeling at ease.

"Are you working on a school project together?" Mrs. Foster asked.

"Not exactly," Larry responded, "but it is a research project. I'll tell you more later. We're in a hurry." The boys bounded up the stairs.

In just a few minutes, they were looking at the results of the Google search. "Frederick Warren, teacher and author . . ."

"Do you think this is the same one as your grandfather?" Larry asked excitedly. "Let's go to the Web site here." Dave watched in hopeful silence as his friend navigated through cyberspace. "Here's a contact site. What should I say?"

Carefully the boys worded a request. "I am searching for my grandfather, Frederick Warren. My mother's name was Mary and she married David Lister on June 4, 1988. Since my mother died, my father has cut off contact with her parents, but I would like to find them. Your help would be appreciated. Please reply at my friend's e-mail address: LarryF@yahoo.com. Sincerely, Dave Lister Jr."

It was with excitement as the boys bounded down the stairs to rejoin Jodi and Cheryl. But the girls were enjoying each other's company, talking and laughing; and the boys, wanting to conceal their excitement, joined in with the conversation.

Mrs. Foster looked on, also enjoying the high spirits of the young people. "I have a proposal to make," Mrs. Foster broke into the fun. "Our family is going camping this weekend at Paradise Campground on the coast. Would Dave and Jodi like to join our family for the outing?"

"I'd love to," Dave said, "but I'll have to ask my dad."

"Of course, you both will need to ask your parents," Mrs. Foster replied. "All you'll need is warm clothes for camping. We have enough tents and sleeping bags unless you prefer your own. We'll be leaving Friday after school, and coming back on Sunday afternoon."

"That would be so cool if you could come!" Cheryl said excitedly to Jodi. Everyone gathered at the back door as they prepared to leave.

Larry looked at his mother and explained, "I promised Jodi I'd get her home before her mother got there. I'll be right back." Mrs. Foster nodded as Dave and Jodi waved good-bye.

Jodi balanced on Larry's bike for the ride home. She bubbled with excitement about the weekend camping trip. When the bike stopped in front of Jodi's apartments, Larry spoke. "You haven't had much of a chance to use ORB lately. I brought them along, in case you wanted to talk to J-gette." He reached in his shirt pocket and brought out the glowing case.

Jodi's eyes and smile were the answer. "Yes, yes! I want to find out about the surprise silver piece I found under my pillow this morning! Do you want to come in while I use them?"

"No, I need to get home. Just take good care of them. I'll get them tomorrow after school." He watched Jodi disappear into the building.

* * *

The campground was bustling with activity when the Foster family arrived Friday evening. They could hear ocean waves pounding on the sand and gulls calling out in the distance. Evergreen trees towered over campsites as campers set up their tents. The ocean air smelt clean and fresh. Mr. Foster directed the setting up of their tents in a semicircle around the fire pit. Mrs. Foster organized the camp kitchen and put the tablecloth on the camp table.

"Why don't we walk down to the beach and watch the sun set," Mr. Foster invited.

"And then we'll come back and eat supper," chimed in Mrs. Foster.

"Last one there is a blue jellyfish!" Cheryl yelled, breaking into a trot. Jodi, Dave, and Larry responded to the challenge, and the race was on. The four friends were pretty evenly matched, and all skidded to a halt at the water's edge at approximately the same time. Panting, they watched as the sun sank lower and lower in the sky, painting the bundles of ribbed clouds with gold, orange, and red colors.

"What a show nature has given us!" Mrs. Foster exclaimed. "But I'm getting hungry. Is anyone else with me?"

"We're right with you, Mom," Larry rubbed his stomach as proof.

They made their way back toward the camp. Stopping at the road between the beach and their campground, an old, blue, Ford pickup passed. The boys thought they recognized a familiar face inside. They exchanged knowing looks.

"Is that who I think it is?" Larry gasped.

"If it's not, it must be a twin sister," Dave fumed. "We sure don't want her to wreck our wonderful time here."

"Who are you talking about?" Cheryl asked curiously.

"Your double-crossing friend, Winnie," said Larry with feeling. "Maybe we'll be lucky enough to avoid her."

Soon the family and friends were roasting hot dogs, sipping soup, and munching on goodies Mrs. Foster had packed. The lantern gave a nice light. The campfire glowed warmly. Flames played hide-and-seek among the blackened logs. Marshmallows would puff up and turn beige at the end of the roasting sticks. Occasionally, one would catch fire and turn black. It was fun to laugh and discuss everyone's roasting skills.

An owl hooted in the distance. "What's that noise?" Jodi asked warily.

"Just a night bird," Larry grinned. "We'll keep you safe from all the camping critters!"

* * *

Larry and Dave awoke the next morning when they heard Mr. Foster building a campfire, and smelled the hotcakes and eggs that Mrs. Foster was making. The girls were still snuggled in their warm sleeping bags.

"Why don't you boys take the first shift in the breakfast queue," suggested Mrs. Foster.

"Don't mind if I do," Larry grinned sleepily, scratching his head and replacing the baseball cap back on his rumpled hair. He and Dave sat at the table while Mrs. Foster stacked steaming hotcakes on their plates. "We'd like to explore the beach before it gets too crowded," Larry announced. "We want to find the treasures first!"

Mr. Foster laughed. "I understand completely," he said. "If I weren't busy tending the campfire, I would be out there, too! I wish you success."

"But," Mrs. Foster piped up, "before you go, brush your teeth and comb your hair!"

"Mom," Larry groaned. "We're camping! I can just wear my baseball cap."

"Don't forget you have guests that have to look at you," Mrs. Foster smiled, thinking warmly of Jodi. She was such a nice girl. She was glad that Cheryl had someone so good for a friend, and Larry seemed attracted to her as well.

* * *

The boys noticed that the beach was not too crowded when they made their way through the sand. But there were a couple of people flying kites, and another couple digging for clams. A lady jogged past them with her black dog.

"Let's find a quiet place by ourselves," Larry suggested as they plodded along the beach. "What I really want to do is talk to L-mor. I haven't had a chance for a day or so."

"Oh, did you bring ORB?" Dave wanted to know.

"Of course," Larry grinned, pulling the green case from an inside pocket in his jacket.

"Super!" said Dave, as he scanned the beach. "See that big rock over there? No one is around that, and it'll give us a little protection."

The boys made their way to the rock, occasionally stepping over decaying seaweed, crab legs, and broken shells. They found a little ledge on one side of the rock just the right height for a seat. Larry opened ORB's case and lifted the mangled glasses out. "Do you want to use them first?" Larry offered.

"No, you go ahead," Dave said.

As Larry lifted the glasses to his eyes, he saw L-mor and D-go at once. "Good morning," L-mor greeted him. "I'm so excited to talk to you now that you've found the Oracles. You have no idea how important this is for you. Study it diligently. It will give you extra strength in fighting the suggestions of the evil angels. It will help you make right choices."

"The Oracles is such a big book, and there's so much to read. Where should I start?" Larry asked.

"If I were you," L-mor began, "I'd start with the book called *Matthew.* It's the story of how the Good One (whose earthly name is God) allowed his son, Guerdon (whose earthly name is Jesus), to come to earth. He disguised himself as a human, to teach earthlings how to belong to the God's kingdom. While he was here, his enemy, Hesperus (who is called the devil by earthlings), tried his best to defeat Jesus. The legion of discouragement tried and tried to tangle him in their webs. The legion of distrust tempted him to doubt his mission and give up. Hesperus disguised himself and tried to get Guerdon to trust in him instead of the Good One. It was a terrible struggle, but he was not defeated. He always chose what was good. Because of Guerdon's victory, the war will be won. It's an awesome story, one the human mind could never invent. It's a story that's hard to believe, but it's true! Just read, read, read, and discover for yourself!"

"Thanks, I'll do that," Larry responded.

Just then, D-go came forward and motioned to speak. "I have a message for my *kanana*, Dave. May I please speak to him?"

"Sure," Larry said, as he removed the glasses and handed them to Dave.

"Greetings, beloved! (That's what your name means!)," D-go said as he put his arm around Dave and gave him a hug. "I see you have found the family Bible in your house. I am thrilled, and it is going to bless you beyond your highest dreams. It is another step on your journey to freedom." D-go's eyes danced as he held out a small shiny piece. "I could hardly wait to give this to you. It's for your k-sun. It's another foundation piece."

Dave felt for the chain around his neck and pulled his k-sun into the sunlight. Smiling, he snapped the newest silver piece in place.

"Be patient," D-go continued. "Your story will be one that causes much rejoicing in the kingdom of the Good One. Keep pursuing all that is in that Bible, as if your life depended on it."

"I will, I will," Dave's voice was full of conviction.

"And now, we have a surprise for you and Larry," D-go clapped his hands excitedly.

Chapter 12

Trip to R-dor

"A surprise?" Dave questioned as he looked through the cracked lenses of ORB and repeated the words of his angel, D-go. He could hardly believe what he was hearing. Wasn't it a wonderful treat to have a weekend away from his alcoholic father to spend at the beach with his best friend? What more would his angel have to surprise him with?

"Yes, a surprise," D-go repeated. "We're offering you and Larry a trip to R-dor to visit the capital of the Good One. Would you like to go?" the angel asked and smiled eagerly. "You know, the ORB could use some repairs, and the manufacturer lives in R-dor."

"Well, yes, but how is it possible?" Dave asked. "Do we need to tell Larry's folks where we're going?"

"It's not necessary," D-go explained. "When we travel in the fifth dimension, time is just seconds in earthly time. It will be so short, you won't be missed."

When Dave explained D-go's invitation to Larry, he did not hesitate. "Wow, that's awesome. What do we need to do?"

L-mor touched Larry's eyes, and immediately, he could see in the fifth dimension. "I see you've got an adventuresome spirit today! Let's join hands," the golden angel instructed.

With anticipation, and trusting their angel's words, Dave and Larry joined hands, and then felt themselves rising from the ground. As they flew past a kite, they looked back at the beach and the man at the end of the kite string. He dropped the string, began pointing at the flying boys, and shouting something they could not understand! In a second, he was out of sight, but the boys laughed. They must have looked pretty strange to that man! Two boys holding hands and flying past his kite!

What a sensation to be rising like this, leaving their world behind! Suddenly a tremendous roar startled them. It was the sound of evil angels zooming in for an attack. The war between the Good One's forces and Hesperus's angels was more real than a scary movie. Apparently Leo and his evil legion did not want humans to see the capital of R-dor, and they surrounded Dave, Larry, and their protective angels. The evil angels seemed to be everywhere, shooting their darts of fear. Their mean eyes pierced and sliced the boys' hope and courage into lifeless corpses.

"Abba, help!" L-mor and D-go cried a desperate prayer. Quickly they touched the hearts on their foreheads. They hoped that help would arrive in time. The little group seemed crushed with the weight of evil upon them, and the boys could hardly breathe. "This is so scary, but I will believe L-mor's words," Larry whispered to convince himself.

Even though L-mor and D-go were strong, they were committed to holding on to their *kananas* with one hand, leaving only one arm for active defense. The struggle continued, tossing them first one way and then another. Evil angels pulled at D-go and L-mor, trying to separate them from the boys. They lunged and kicked and dove into their targets. Just when it seemed the little group was doomed, a bright blinding light shone all around them, and shouts of victory chorused in their ears. Help from the Good One had arrived just in time, and Leo and his gang were forced to leave, retreating angrily, shaking their fists, beating themselves in disgust, and shouting curses.

Now, the little group was encouraged as they were surrounded by the angels of light. There was a group hug, and then amid smiles and laughter, they were pushed upward, as if a balloon was being pushed into the air by playing children. Dave and Larry could hear the angels wishing them well for the trip. What a send-off!

They were flying higher and higher, their speed increasing every moment. The earth grew smaller and smaller, and the sky became darker and darker. The stars were brilliant against the black sky.

And the little group of travelers began to glow with a soft light. As their speed increased, the starlights seemed to streak by. "Wow, it looks like falling stars!" Larry exclaimed, "but we're the ones that are falling, or rising, I should say!"

L-mor smiled. "Would you like to fly through a comet tail?" And suddenly they came upon a comet. "Here we go, right through the small stuff, but watch out for the big ones . . ." The shining particles of the tail passed right through them. The only sensation they felt were little tickles waving through their bodies, and lighting them up as if a light bulb were passing through.

"How funny," Dave chuckled with glee! "You look like a Christmas tree, Larry! And look at how the particles swirl after they've left us!" This trip through space was more than these two earthlings had ever imagined.

"Let's do a forward loop," D-go said playfully. "Everyone lean forward!" As they leaned forward, D-go and L-mor swung their arms back and down to give them the momentum. Over everyone went, as if the foursome was in slow motion, and then back up to their former position.

"I like to do the spin," L-mor said. "Here we go!" He flew toward D-go and took his hand. The motion started them spinning in a circle, all the while moving forward. The boys were laughing with pleasure.

"I've never been on a carnival ride this exciting," Larry laughed. Then something caught his ear. "What's that? Do I hear music coming from somewhere? It's cooler than anything I've ever heard."

"We're nearing R-dor," L-mor explained. "See that bright light ahead. It's the sights and sounds of your future home when the war is over."

Now the boys focused on the dazzling light ahead of them, growing larger and larger with each passing moment. The light was like a huge prism, reflecting all colors of the rainbow. As they grew closer, the shape came into focus. R-dor appeared to be round, like other celestial bodies they had seen, but the light of it was different. One area of crystal blue light seemed to draw their attention. As they flew closer, they could see that this was the capital city, with translucent blue walls. Through the walls they could see the buildings sparkling like gold. There were huge gates open for the residents to pass in and out. Near each gate was a waterfall. "We will pass through the waterfall," D-go instructed. "We must wash the pollution of earth from us before we enter the city." The waterfall felt refreshing, and as they flew out of the water, the boys were amazed to see that their clothes had miraculously changed into the glowing golden garments of R-dor!

Inside the city were beautiful buildings and streets covered with gold and sparkling with precious stones. There were parks and waterways with greenery and flowers lovelier than they had ever seen. This was so awesome. And yet, Larry and Dave were so amazed, they were speechless. L-mor and D-go led them along the main boulevard. There was so much to see, one could scarcely take it in.

"There is someone special we want you to meet," D-go said. "Here, we call him Guerdon, but in your Bibles, he is called Jesus. It is because of him you will be able to one day stay here if you want to." They entered a magnificent building, and as they entered what seemed to be a throne room, the light was so blinding, the boys had to bow their heads and squint their eyes almost closed to be comfortable. They caught glimpses of myriads of angels and shining creatures with lots of eyes and wings moving in rhythm to singing that was indescribably lovely.

"Come, my messengers and earthly children," a strong but friendly voice invited them. L-mor and D-go led their *kananas* toward the voice. The youths felt a firm hand on their shoulders, and felt power surging from that touch throughout their bodies. "You are special to me," the voice said. "I can hardly wait until you can be here with my 'Abba' and me all the time. Until then, be strong for me, and remember, I am always with you. I will strengthen you."

"Thank you, thank you," the boys chorused feebly, still not able to open their eyes and look. L-mor and D-go led their charges out of the building to the boulevard once more. Slowly their eyes adjusted to their surroundings.

While everyone they met seemed to have a task to do, there was happiness and playfulness permeating everywhere. L-mor stopped in a little shop along the way. "Here we are at the ORB House," he said as he led them all inside. "O-pra will help us."

It was not a large room they entered, but well lit with glittering shelves along one wall. The shelves were filled with different varieties of ORBs. On another wall was a marble counter, with several pots of steaming liquid and a variety of work tools. The third wall was covered in shining silver, with names engraved there.

A friendly voice greeted them. "Oh, I see there is a problem here," the smiling angel in attendance observed. "It will just take a moment to fix these." She gently removed the glasses and dipped them in one of the pots where the mist was rising. When the glasses came out, the cracks were gone. O-pra gently waved the glasses in front of a fanlike device to dry them off. Mysteriously, the bent frames straightened by themselves. "There you are, just as good as new," she said with a smile.

She handed the glasses to Dave, and then approached the silver wall. She touched a name. It was then they realized that the name she had touched was theirs. But the name had been so scratched and marred, it was hardly readable. When O-pra touched their name, the cracks disappeared, and it could now be read easily. "There, the record wall is updated. This wall lists my earthlings with ORBs, and now it is all in order," she smiled. "Go in peace!"

"Thank you," Dave waved good-bye.

L-mor and D-go led them out the door and down the boulevard. They paused in front of another building, shimmering with sparkling silver. "This is where the k-suns are made, but I don't want to take you inside," L-mor grinned. "I don't want to spoil your surprise!"

"Oh," chorused Dave and Larry, their eyes sparkling with anticipation and curiosity.

D-go smiled and pretended to ignore their interest in the k-sun building. Instead, he paused at a building built of crystal. "This is where the invisible garments are woven. It's like a toy shop for us angels." A mischievous grin played at his lips. They could see the angels inside, working the cream-colored thread on a large loom. Other angels were spinning a large vat of steaming liquid. Cream-colored thread rose from the center of the vat onto a large spool. Other angels were shaping the garments and putting the finishing touches on them. One wall was lined with shelves of cream-colored garments.

Just then, a lively new song of music filled the air. "The musicians are providing the atmosphere of joy and happiness," L-mor explained. "The music hall is just across the boulevard over there. The music waves radiate out over R-dor and inspire us all, giving us energy so we work well."

As they continued down the boulevard, the buildings ended and they could see that they were coming to another boulevard. Across that boulevard was a large open area like a beautiful park dotted with trees and flowering shrubs. A crystal clear river ran in front of them, and they saw the most amazing tree they had ever seen. It was so large it looked like a series of trees all joined at the top. Its tall graceful branches were filled with sparkling fruit of all colors. The tree was also wide, with fruit-filled branches extending to the ground so angels could pick the fruit and eat it.

L-mor and D-go picked some fruit. "We eat this each day," D-go explained. "It has properties that keep us alive and healthy. We call this tree the Tree of Life. We thought we might as well get our piece while we're here. Sorry we can't share with you yet, but someday, you will be able to taste it too when the war is over."

Just then, a bright yellow bird with iridescent purple wings landed on Dave's shoulder. It opened its little beak and warbled its song.

"It's tame!" Larry exclaimed, reaching up to touch its soft feathers.

"All the creatures are tame here. There is nothing to harm them, and there is no fear," L-mor murmured.

"Oh, here comes the watch-bug," D-go held out his hand for a glittering insect with multiple wings and a happy little face. It rubbed some wings together, and it made the ticking sound of a watch. "He's coming to tell us that our allotted time with you in R-dor is almost over. There's a lot more to see, but we must go back to earth now."

* * *

The trip back to earth was just as spectacular as their trip leaving earth. At last they found themselves on the beach in Oregon. At one time, they thought this was a very special place. But after seeing the wonders of R-dor, the beach seemed plain and dreary.

"Before we say good-bye," L-mor smiled, "I want to give you something, Larry. The takeoff on our trip today was hazardous, meeting Leo's team. But you overcame your fear with trust in Good One's promises. Here is another piece for your k-sun." He held out a shiny silver piece.

"Thank you," Larry responded eagerly. He examined the piece and fitted it in the proper place on the k-sun's frame. "It's starting to look like a strong fort!"

"And thank you for the nice trip and all," Dave added. He thoughtfully placed the "good as new" ORB back in its case. Larry and Dave sat in silence on the rock, watching the waves and pondering the things they had just witnessed. It seemed like they had been gone from this spot for hours, but yet, the same people were flying kites and digging for clams just as it was before the trip to R-dor.

At last the ocean breezes, the pounding surf, and the seagulls playing tug-of-war with some morsel they had found beckoned to the boys and coaxed them back to reality. "Let's go down to those rocks over there, and see if there's something caught in the tide pools," Dave suggested.

"That's right," Larry remembered. "I did tell my folks that we were going to hunt for treasures! I had no idea we'd see the treasures of R-dor!"

When they returned to camp a few hours later, they had collected a few sand dollars and shells. But best of all, they had found a glass bottle with a piece of paper inside. As they walked into the campsite, they found Larry's dad whittling on a piece of wood. "Dad, we found something really cool, but we can't get the cork out. Can you help us?" Larry asked.

"Well, well," Mr. Foster said, turning the bottle over a couple of times for examination. "You did indeed find a treasure! Let's see what we can do here. Maybe this bottle has come all the way from China! Maybe it was swallowed by a whale and spat out on the beach! Maybe it was thrown off a pirate ship just off shore!" The boys grinned at Mr. Foster's lame jokes, but they were curious how far this bottle had traveled.

"Well, with my luck," Dave said with a smile, "it was probably left by some camper last week!"

"I have a corkscrew somewhere in my kitchen gadget box," Mrs. Foster offered as she searched among the cooking utensils in the plastic container.

"Perfect," Mr. Foster responded, as he took the tool to remove the cork. "This was sure stuck in there tight." He handed the bottle back to the boys. Larry turned the bottle upside down and shook it, but the fold in the paper prevented it from entering the neck of the bottle. Dave found a stick and began poking inside the bottle.

At last, he managed to drag the note through the narrow opening. Larry quickly snatched the note from Dave.

The note was handwritten with a name and address, and then a message written in a foreign language. Mrs. Foster looked at it in astonishment. Seeing the address, she gasped, "It's come all the way from the Philippines. I think it's written in Spanish."

Then Mr. Foster inspected it and made out the word "Senior," but there were no other words that looked familiar. It was a mystery that could only be solved when they found a translator. Perhaps someone from Mr. or Mrs. Foster's workplace could help them. "If you can part with this piece of paper," Mr. Foster said, "I'll take it to work with me and see if someone there can translate it. If it has come thousands of miles across the ocean, I think we want to know what it says." Larry nodded in agreement, and Mr. Foster folded the paper and put it in his wallet for safekeeping.

"By the way," Mrs. Foster interrupted. "Have you seen the girls? They left after breakfast to go for a walk, and it's almost time for lunch."

"Didn't see them on the beach," Larry responded. "Would you like us to go look for them?"

"Please do," Mrs. Foster said. "They headed that way," she pointed toward the campground road.

The boys headed off in the direction Mrs. Foster had pointed. The campground was designed with four loops, and Larry and Dave walked down the middle loop. There were campsites at the beginning of the loop, and then a grouping of cabins at the far end of the loop. "Here's that blue pickup we saw last night," mumbled Dave as they passed a cabin. "There's another car, too. She must be with some friends."

"Let's hurry along, then," Larry replied, picking up his pace. He wanted to avoid Winnie if at all possible. At a space near the end of the loop, a hiking trail wended its way into a forest of old growth trees. "Do you think they would have taken the trail?"

"Maybe," Dave replied. Turning into the path, the giant trees towered over them. On the lower branches, moss hung in wispy clumps. The trail seemed quiet and lonely with few people choosing its solitude when the bombastic waves of the ocean were just over the next ridge. Larry and Dave hurried along, wondering if Cheryl and

Jodi would have chosen this path. Before long, the forest opened into a grassland dotted with scrubby trees. Small songbirds called to each other and flitted from one dwarf evergreen to another. The path became sandy and turned toward the ocean.

"This is probably the way they went," Larry encouraged. They climbed the path to the top of the dune, and there was the ocean before them. As far as their eyes could see, the azure blue waves were washing ashore, frosted with strips of white foam. It would be nice to pause and enjoy the picture in front of them, but their mission urged them on. They scanned the beach for the girls. Larry pointed to two figures, "Is that them?"

"I can't tell," Dave responded moving forward as fast as he could. As the boys got closer to the girls, they were disappointed to see that they were strangers. Larry and Dave continued down the beach, heading toward the campground. "Maybe they're ahead of us and are back at camp already," Dave suggested hopefully.

"That would be a good thing!" Larry exclaimed. He had hoped to spend more time with Jodi this weekend. Back at the camp, they were disappointed that the girls still had not returned. "Let's check the other campground loops," Larry suggested, and the boys trotted off, but returned without success.

"I don't like this," Mr. Foster said with a worried look on his face. "I hope the girls are not in some kind of trouble. I'm going to check at the camp office and see if the warden has seen them. And I'll check the park entrance while I'm there."

While Mr. Foster was gone, Mrs. Foster urged the boys to eat something. "You must be starved by now," she said.

Sensing her urgency, they gulped down their food, as soldiers in the trenches might do. "I've got an idea," Larry whispered. "Remember ORB has a fast-forward. Do you think we ought to use it?" Dave's eyes responded, "Yes!"

Larry and Dave retreated into their tent. Larry carefully put ORB to his eyes and pushed the FF button. It wasn't long before a startling scene unfolded before his eyes. Larry sighed and removed the glasses. "L-mor told me it was best to stop looking, but I did see us approaching Winnie's cabin. There were evil angels (Leo's group that attacked us this morning) surrounding it. L-mor told me that Cheryl and Jodi are trapped inside."

"Oh no!" Dave groaned. He shrank from the thought of the force and brutality that Leo's legion used. "Can we say D-go's prayer, 'help Abba'?"

"It can't hurt," Larry murmured, putting ORB back in its case. "I know L-mor and D-go will be with us. And this morning, Guerdon promised to give us strength. But I think we ought to wait for Dad to come back to go with us."

"Good idea!" Dave responded. "Your dad is a cool man."

A half hour later, Mr. Foster returned, a worried expression still on his face. "Have they returned?" he asked. He could see the answer on everyone's gloomy faces.

"Dad," Larry said. "I have a strong hunch we need to inquire at a cabin down this loop. We think we recognized one of Cheryl's not-so-good friends coming in to the campground last night. Her pickup is parked there. I don't get along very well with her friend, Winnie, so would appreciate your help."

"Sure," Mr. Foster agreed. "Let's go!"

All was quiet at the cabin when they knocked at the door, but immediately, there was scuffling activity and muffled voices inside. Slowly the door opened a crack, and an impatient voice questioned, "Yes?"

"Sorry to bother you," Mr. Foster began, "but our daughter Cheryl and friend Jodi have disappeared, and we are trying to find them. Have you seen them?"

"How would I know?" the voice responded testily.

"We thought some in your party might know them," Mr. Foster pressed. "Is Winnie here?"

"Oh, let them in," a voice groaned from within. "Yes, Winnie's here, never fear."

The door opened to a darkened room, the floor littered with cartons, empty brown bottles, and the lingering smell of smoke. Winnie was sitting on the floor, her back propped against the bed. "So you're missing Cheryl, are ya?" her voice was slurred.

"Yes, since about ten this morning, and we last saw her walking this way with her friend," Mr. Foster answered. Just then, a banging noise and tussling was heard coming from the bathroom.

"Don't mind my friends," Winnie croaked nervously. "They're awful noisy in the bathroom."

"Sounds like they need some help," Larry piped up. He quickly pushed against the door, which he forced to open a crack and then it slammed shut again and locked. "They're in there," Larry shouted. "I saw them!"

"You're crazy mistaken," Winnie cooed. "Don't be rude to my friends in the bathroom. Just leave them be, and go looking somewhere else for your poor lost sister."

"I'm sorry," Mr. Foster said sternly, "but I saw the girls in there too, and either your friends release them, or I will contact the security officers. They have already been alerted that the girls are missing." He pulled his cell phone from his pocket.

"Sorry, dude," said Winnie, "but that cell phone won't work out here in the wilderness. You're out of luck. You better leave, now."

"I think we *are* in luck," Dave shouted with relief. "The security officers just drove up!"

In a matter of minutes, the girls were rescued from the bathroom. Their hands and feet had been tied, and mouths gagged. Two rough-looking characters emerged with them, and the officers handcuffed them and forced them against the wall. There were looks of relief as Larry and Dave removed the ropes from the girls' wrists and ankles.

The security officers radioed for the state police. Within a short time, the officers arrived and began questioning Winnie and her friends. They also questioned Mr. Foster and the young people for a complete report. Eventually the Fosters and friends were told they could go back to their camp while Winnie and her friends were arrested and removed from camp.

Back at the Fosters' camp, there were hugs all around, and tears of relief and joy. As the story unfolded, Winnie had invited the girls inside her cabin, hoping they would join in the party. When the girls refused, Winnie's friends tried to force them and refused to let them go until they had smoked or drunk.

"We were sure glad to hear your voices at the door, believe me," said Jodi. Her eyes rested on Larry, and the admiration for him that shone there touched him with a tenderness that made him feel good all over. "I don't know what would have happened next if you hadn't come," her voice trailed off.

"Whatever made you look for us there?" Cheryl asked.

"It was just a hunch," Larry said, giving Jodi a knowing look. "I'll tell you about it sometime."

Chapter 13

The Visitors

Tiger, the cat, was waiting at the door when the family arrived home from their camping trip. He scolded them persistently, until one by one, each family member had picked him up and comforted him from the trauma of spending a weekend alone at home. A big helping of treats was placed in his food dish, and that seemed to soothe him. Soon he was galloping around the house in play, as if begging someone to play tag or hide-and-seek with him.

When the chores were completed, Larry eagerly retreated to his room. He wanted to spend some time with ORB, talking to L-mor and reviewing their experience with Winnie at the campground. How nice it was to open ORB's case and see its soft glow with no cracks or crimps. Pushing the RW button, he put the green glasses to his eyes. Back at the campground, he saw himself with his dad and friend Dave approaching Winnie's cabin. It was horrible how Leo and his evil angels surrounded the cabin. "They like us," chuckled Leo wickedly, pointing at the cabin. "These puny earthworms have chosen us over the Good One's army, so we can wrap them up in webs as much as we want. They'll just repeat everything we tell them to, without even using their brains."

Inside the cabin Larry spotted Winnie's golden angel, backed into a corner by some of the evil angels. She was shouting, "Don't listen to them. They're bad for you!" But there were so many of the evil angels, and their voices overpowered the good angel. Winnie was obviously pleased with the orders she was receiving from Leo and his gang. Like a parrot in a cage, she repeated everything they were prompting her to say.

When Larry, Dave, and Dad had entered the cabin, Larry saw L-mor and D-go touch the hearts on their foreheads. Immediately more golden angels appeared beside them. He saw them giving him strength and courage to open the bathroom door, where Winnie's prisoners were being held. He saw the angels giving wise words to his dad. He saw them escorting the security officer's car as it arrived at just the right time. But like true gentlemen, they did not interfere with Winnie or her friends' choices. A good angel follows the rules of freedom and will not force a *kanana* who does not want to do what is right. Winnie had chosen Leo and his team over the Good One's team.

Sadly, Larry murmured to L-mor. "Before I got ORB, I had no idea there was such a real battle between good and evil." Then with determination, he said, "I want to always choose the ways of the Good One and his kingdom!"

"You'll never be sorry," L-mor handed Larry a shiny silver piece for his k-sun. "I am proud how strong you were to help me with the girls' rescue. Now, check your e-mails. I think you'll like what you find!"

"Okay, I will," Larry said, holding up the silver piece. "Thank you!" With a smile and nod from L-mor, Larry removed ORB and put it safely away in his pocket.

Larry turned on his computer. While he was waiting for it to boot up, he attached the new piece to his k-sun. It was starting to look like something more than a wiry framework. Turning back to his computer, he wondered if there was a response to Dave's note to Frederick Warren. Wouldn't it be cool if he were Dave's grandfather? It took the computer forever to boot up, but at last the message came, "You've got mail!"

Yes, there was a message, and Larry read it carefully and slowly.

Dear Dave,

It has been the longing and prayer of our hearts to find you. Yes, we are your grandparents. The rift between your father and us has always saddened us. When your father disappeared with you, leaving no address or information for us to find you, our lives have held an empty spot. Now, the hope of seeing you again, gives us much joy. Please tell us the best way to proceed.

With love, Grandpa and Grandma Warren

Larry was so excited for this good news. He wanted to race right over to Dave's to give him the message, but then again, he didn't want to risk making Dave's father suspicious of him and Dave, and then abuse Dave for something he imagined was wrong. Perhaps he should just print out the letter and give it to Dave at school tomorrow.

The next morning, Larry rode the bus to school, and eagerly greeted Dave when he sat down beside him. Dave was still processing in his mind the events that led up to the beating his father had given him last night. When Larry handed him the letter from his grandfather, it took a few moments for him to realize what was in his hand. When he did, his hands began to tremble, and a lone tear slid down his cheek. "I can't believe it's my grandparents," he spoke with emotion. "This must be why I found another piece to my k-sun in my shoe this morning."

"Congratulations," Larry encouraged, patting his friend on the back. "This is the best news ever. Good One's team is pulling for you, man. After school, you can come up with a game plan."

They met Jodi outside their homeroom. "What's the matter with Dave?" she questioned.

"I just gave him an e-mail letter from his grandparents," Larry said. "It's pretty emotional news for him. And how are you after your rough weekend?"

"I'll be okay," Jodi replied. "These red marks on my wrists don't hurt, and they'll go away in a few days."

"What did your mother say?" Larry's eyes were full of question and sympathy.

"Not much. I'm not sure she even noticed." Jodi's voice sounded sad and she quickly changed the subject. "I bet Winnie is hurting today. The authorities caught them in their mess, for sure. She'll probably have to get drug rehab or whatever the courts say."

Jodi pulled a small black bag from her pocket. It had a zipper on the top. "Could you use something like this to keep ORB's case in? I was thinking it would hide the glow."

"Cool!" Larry took the bag and examined it. "What a clever idea! Now ORB won't be so easy to see. Thanks."

"By the way, how is Cheryl?" Jodi asked.

"She's fine," Larry smiled. "I think she rather enjoyed the excitement and attention once she knew she was safe. And she's learned how far she can trust Winnie, which is a good thing!"

"I'm glad for that. I really like your sister," Jodi added. "I think we should include her on our team. Don't you think you can trust her with ORB by now? She knows you have it."

"I'll have to think about that." Larry still seemed unsure of Cheryl.

* * *

The air was crisp and cool when school dismissed. "Good thing we went camping when we did. It feels like winter is just around the corner," Larry shivered as the coldness enveloped his body.

Dave nodded and began to talk about what was most important to him. "I'd like to discuss this e-mail with your father."

"With Dad?" Larry asked. "Okay, shall we stop by his work and talk to him? The walk home is a little longer than when we take the bus, but he'll be glad to see us."

"Oh, if he wouldn't mind, I would like that." Dave responded eagerly.

When Mr. Foster saw the two boys, he greeted them warmly and led them into his office. Larry never came to his office unless it was really important, so he sensed that something unusual had happened. He noticed the red abrasion on Dave's jaw, and knew that he had suffered at the hand of his father again. Closing the door, he said, "What's up?"

Dave began to talk, slowly at first with much emotion, and then increased in speed as his thoughts became clearer. The details of his story spewed out like soda from a can that had been shaken before being opened. Mr. Foster leaned back in his chair and listened intently, amazed that this young man had suffered so in his short life. The news of the grandparents was a relief. Dave handed the e-mail letter to Mr. Foster to read. "So what do I do next?" Dave asked. "I don't want to ruin everything. My dad can be so jealous."

Mr. Foster thought for a few seconds. "My suggestion would be for you to invite them to come to Warrenville. We could arrange a meeting at our place. You can see if you like each other and want to build a relationship. And if you do want them in your life, Mrs. Foster and I will do everything we can to help with the details of that."

"Oh, thank you," Dave murmured. A look of relief and peace settled over him.

"Jodi's mom works at a motel," Larry suggested. "Maybe your grandparents could stay there when they come." A trace of a smile formed on Dave's face as he saw the puzzle pieces fitting together. He so wanted everything to work out well and yet the fear of the past made him cautious.

When the boys arrived at Larry's home, Mrs. Foster was just arriving home from work. The boys eagerly shared the events that were about to take place. "I also have an idea to add," she said. "You know, Larry is having a birthday in a couple of weeks. If your grandparents could come around that time, we could have a little family party to celebrate two things! And Dave's dad would not be so suspicious of him spending time here!"

"That's a splendid idea, Mom!" Larry was enthusiastic. A party in his honor felt good, and even more rewarding if it were combined with such a special event for his best friend. Larry and Dave bounded upstairs to the computer so Dave could compose a letter to his grandparents.

They had not been there long when there was a tap on the door. "May I come in?" Cheryl's voice called.

"Sure, come in," Larry responded. "We're just writing a letter to Dave's grandparents."

"That's so cool," Cheryl joined in the happy events that were unfolding. "By the way, you've never told me how you knew where to find us when Winnie's friends took us prisoner."

Larry hesitated, and then spoke quickly, "Remember the green glasses? My angel told me."

Cheryl's eyes opened wide with astonishment. "Your angel?"

"You've heard of guardian angels, haven't you?" Larry asked. "When I wear the green glasses, I can see my angel and hear him talking to me."

Cheryl grew silent as she recalled the one time she had tried on the green glasses. "What does your angel look like?"

"He's short and fat and jolly with a red heart on his forehead. He wears a golden bodysuit."

"Golden suit?" Cheryl questioned. "The day I tried the glasses on, I saw one in a camouflage suit."

"That was an enemy angel. They're bad news." Larry turned back to the computer and Dave.

Cheryl silently left the room, deep in thought.

* * *

In a few days, all the arrangements had been made for Dave to meet his grandparents. In their letters, Mr. and Mrs. Warren seemed thrilled to connect with their long-lost grandson. Dave was excited but also afraid to hope that someone could love him for who he was and make him feel safe. His life had been so hard with his alcoholic and unpredictable father.

While Dave, Larry, and Jodi waited for the special day to arrive, they talked to their angels daily. What a gift ORB was to them! L-mor and D-go continued to encourage them and give them hope. In addition to that, they also helped their *kananas* understand things they were reading in the Oracles. "You can also help us win the world for the Good One," suggested L-mor. "Every time you encourage one of our *kananas* to do what is right or help them heal from their discouragements, you are boosting the cause of the Good One. You are also untangling the webs that the evil angels are using to try to capture earthlings."

* * *

At last Larry's birthday arrived. Mrs. Foster stayed home from work that afternoon, to prepare food and decorate the family room. She had Mylar balloons that looked like huge baseballs, and hung up decorative cutouts of baseball bats on the walls. The cake was also decorated with the baseball theme. She was pleased with the effect, and then turned her attention to the living room. This was where Dave would meet his grandparents. She made sure everything was in order. She hoped for Dave's sake that this would be a positive experience.

About an hour before the youth were expected home, Mr. Foster arrived with Dave's grandparents. Mr. Warren was a distinguished-looking man with a kindly face. Mrs. Warren was plump and jolly.

"Would you care for drinks?" Mr. Foster offered. He led his guests to the living room, and everyone sat down.

"We thought it would be good to get acquainted before Dave gets here. He has been a friend to our son since third grade, so we know him well. He is a very good young man and in a most unfortunate situation with his father."

"We're sorry to hear that," Mr. Warren said. "Somehow we suspected that. Tell us more."

Mr. Foster shared the struggles he had seen Dave go through, the marks and bruises on his face when his father beat him. He noted that Dave always wore long sleeves and long pants to cover up any other marks that he may have received at the hand of his father.

"We are prepared to help in any way we can, even if it means moving to Warrenville to be closer to our grandson," Mrs. Warren said.

"I'm sure Dave would be thrilled if that happened," Mrs. Foster responded.

The conversation continued comfortably until they heard voices at the back door. Mrs. Foster rose to usher Dave, Larry, Cheryl, and Jodi into the living room. Taking Dave gently by the arm, she said, "Dave, I'd like to introduce you to your grandparents, Mr. and Mrs. Warren."

"And this is our son Larry, and daughter Cheryl," Mr. Foster chimed in, "and another special friend, Jodi."

"Pleased to meet you all," the Warrens chorused as they nodded and rose to their feet. Their gaze was drawn back to Dave. Mr. Warren extended his hand warmly, but Mrs. Warren opened her arms wide and engulfed Dave in a warm hug. Dave turned red, but a pleased smile crept over his face. He wasn't used to being fussed over, but it felt good.

"I know I'm terribly embarrassing to a young man like you," Mrs. Warren bubbled, "but I'm just so glad to see you at last, I can't help myself!" She drew Dave to a seat near them. "We want to know all about you."

"And you may have a lot of questions to ask us!" Mr. Warren added.

"We'll leave you three to get better acquainted," Mrs. Foster said. "I could use the rest of you in the kitchen to help get the final touches ready for our celebration."

When the meal was ready, everyone gathered in the family room. The good smells made everyone eager to eat. "We are so happy for this occasion that brings us all together," Mrs. Foster smiled and turned to her son. "Larry, as our birthday man, will you please lead the way to the food and show Dave and his grandparents where to find the goodies?"

When the meal was over, and the candles on the birthday cake were blown out, Mrs. Foster announced, "It's time for presents!" Larry grinned with anticipation. He had noticed one gift behind all the others that really made him curious. And he was not disappointed. There were many nice gifts, but that special box held a Play Station 3. All of the young people were excited about that, and eager to use it with Larry. "Let's wait until later with that," requested Mrs. Foster. "I think Mr. and Mrs. Warren have a celebration gift for Dave."

A look of astonishment crept over Dave's face. "A gift for me?" he thought. He seldom got gifts for his birthday, and this was not even his birthday. He tore off the paper and opened the box. He could hardly believe what he saw. It was a laptop computer!

"We wanted you to have your very own computer," Mr. Warren said, "so we can e-mail each other."

"Thank you," Dave mumbled, overcome with emotion. "I don't know what to say! Thank you." He tapped his head to make sure he was not dreaming, blinked his eyes, smiled, and then turned to give his grandparents a hug.

"Let me help you get it set up," Mr. Warren offered.

"And let's set up the Play Station for Larry," Mr. Foster suggested.

As the young people were enjoying the new gifts, Mr. Foster asked a question. "Mr. and Mrs. Warren, how long do you folks plan to spend in town?"

"A few more days," came the reply. "We want to check on a few things and spend a little more time with Dave before we head back to California."

"That sounds good." Mr. Foster nodded his approval. "You are welcome to use our place for headquarters if you need to."

"Thanks," Mr. Warren said. "We're hoping we can take Dave out to eat tomorrow evening. We'll see if Dave can arrange that!"

* * *

Dave had a very sober expression when he stopped by the motel the next afternoon.

"What's wrong, my lad?" Mr. Warren questioned, as he invited Dave into their room. "Were you able to arrange time with us this evening without making your father angry?"

"Oh yes," Dave replied. "Dad is working the late shift tonight. He doesn't know I'm here. It's my new computer that I'm worried about," Dave replied. "Dad found it last night and accused me of stealing it and then threw it outside. I think it hit a tree before it landed on the ground. It's sort of broken."

"Have a seat, Dave," Mr. Warren said. "Let's have a look at it." Dave was obviously in pain. Very slowly and carefully he sat down. "He must have hurt you, too," Mr. Warren continued, noticing the grimace on Dave's face. He nodded slowly.

Mr. Warren opened the computer case. "These things can be pretty tough," he said. "Let's see if it comes on . . . nope, doesn't look like it. Let's leave it here for now, and I'll work some more on it tomorrow."

"I'm really sorry," Dave apologized. "I don't know why my dad gets so mad sometimes."

"I'm sorry, too," Mr. Warren said. "But I'm sorrier that you're hurt. Would you be willing to come with me to the emergency room to get examined?"

"I don't think my dad would like it," Dave hesitated.

"Perhaps he won't like it, Dave," Mr. Warren said. "But if he hurt you badly, that is wrong. And we need to stop him from doing this to you. Please come with me," he coaxed.

"Okay," Dave agreed reluctantly. A small silver piece tinkled to the floor. Dave stooped to pick it up and smiled with surprise. It was another piece for his k-sun. Dave placed the silver piece in his shirt pocket. He would attach it later.

Mr. Warren hadn't noticed the silver piece, or realized what was happening. Instead, he responded to the serious decision Dave had made. "That's a smart lad. It will be for the best." Apparently D-go had approved of his decision as well. He felt the k-sun in his pocket and was encouraged.

At the hospital, the doctor wore a serious expression as he examined Dave. The wounds from the beating were bad. They needed bandages and treatment. The doctor questioned Dave about his father's anger and rage when he punished Dave. Dave was reluctant to tell, but knowing he now had grandparents to help him, it gave Dave courage. He told the truth.

When the examination and treatment were over, the doctor asked to speak to Mr. Warren alone. He told Mr. Warren that he needed to submit a report to the authorities about the injuries. In a few minutes, Grandpa Warren was back, and they walked toward the car.

"Now we have a surprise for you. We want to show you something on our way to the restaurant." There was a twinkle in Grandpa's eyes, and Grandma was smiling broadly. In a few minutes, they were driving past the neighborhood where the grand old houses were located. Mr. Warren stopped the car in front of a large home. A "For Sale" sign was standing in the front lawn. "This is the home where my father was raised. His family (his grandparents and great-grandparents) came to this place in the early days. My Grandpa owned a large department store, and his family was quite important to this town—in fact, they named the town after his family, W*arrenville*."

"I didn't know that!" said Dave in surprise.

Grandpa Warren continued, "Your grandma and I talked to the realtor today, and we are going to buy this old home back for our family and move here. Then we will be close and can help you with your computer problems or whatever else happens, or if your father hurts you again."

Chapter 14

The Big Bang

Mr. Foster came bouncing through the door. "I've got a message for you. I've got a message for you!" he sang loudly.

The family began to gather around him in the family room. "What's all the fuss about?" Mrs. Foster questioned.

"Remember the message in the bottle that the boys found at the beach?" Mr. Foster searched the eyes of his audience. "I've found someone to translate it."

"What is it? Tell us," Larry pleaded in excitement.

"Your clever mother was right." Mr. Foster winked at his wife. "This is written in Spanish. It comes from the Philippines, clear on the other side of the Pacific Ocean. It was written about two years ago by a girl who was twelve years old. Here is what she says":

Help me find God. I want to be happy.
Angelina Cortez, age 12, #32 Blanco Road, Manila, Philippines

"What a strange message," Mrs. Foster commented.

"I don't think so," Larry mused.

"What makes you say that?" Mrs. Foster asked.

"Well," Larry wondered how he could answer without telling about ORB and his angel. Then it came to him. "I've been reading the Bible you gave me. It's helping me to understand how this world was made, and who God is. I feel better about my life. And I think God is helping Dave with his life too. I think we're happier."

"That's true about Dave," Mr. Foster commented. "His grandparents' visit was truly a lucky thing for him."

"I think it is more than luck," Larry emphasized. "I think God had a lot to do with it."

"Whatever," Cheryl joined the conversation. "So, Larry, are you going to answer the message from the bottle?"

Larry shrugged his shoulders. "I don't know how to write in Spanish."

"Silly boy," Cheryl smirked. "You can write in English. She can get it translated just like you got hers translated. Or you could use the Web site *babelfish.com*."

"I guess I could," Larry grinned good-naturedly as everyone chuckled. "What's *babelfish*?"

"It's a program to help you translate another language," Cheryl informed him.

"Maybe you'd like to help me?" Larry asked.

"I'm not very good at the subject of God." Cheryl replied. "I think *you* found the bottle, so it's *your* message, right?"

*   *   *

Dave was in good spirits when he got on the bus the next morning. The hope his grandparents had given him made every day a better day. He could hardly wait until they moved to Warrenville. He still had not told his father about finding them. He would wait until they were safely close by before he started that storm.

"You know who I'm feeling sorry for?" Dave asked his friend. Larry turned to listen. "It's Todd. He doesn't have any friends, and when we see him with ORB, those evil angels are really spinning a web on him."

"That's true," Larry said, "but what do you think we can do?"

"I don't know," Dave responded, "maybe try to talk to him more, or ask him to do things with us."

"Good luck," Larry said. "It feels like the freezer door is open when you talk to him."

"We could ask D-go and L-mor next time we talk to them," Dave continued as they walked through the school door.

Larry's attention switched to Jodi, who was walking up to meet them. The mint green sweater she was wearing looked very striking with her hair and eyes. "Hey, guys," she smiled. "Are you ready for the science test today?"

The fake groans made her chuckle. "Seriously, guys! He's going to ask us about how the universe started." In their minds they pictured their science teacher. He was a big man, one who had been a star of his college football team. He wasn't particularly bright, but he had graduated from college and worked hard at drumming the textbook facts into their heads. His motto was to uphold the textbook because it was proven and true—no answers to the right or the left were acceptable.

"So," Jodi continued, "are you going to answer with the Big Bang Theory, which is in our textbook, or are you going to make him mad and say that God started it and made everything, like we read in our Bibles?"

Larry thought for a moment. "I guess I'll have to tell it like I believe it. The Good One had to do it. This universe is too complicated to have happened by itself. Maybe the Good One did it with a Big Bang, but he had to be there! To not stand up for him and his kingdom would be like taking sides with Hesperus and his evil angels."

Dave and Jodi nodded. "I agree," Dave said. "I think our angels will help us write the right thing if we get asked that question."

As they walked into homeroom, the bell rang. Dave noticed Todd sitting at his desk. His head was down on the desk, resting on his arms. He did not stir as Mrs. Crump, the teacher, took the role.

"It's time for your spelling test," Mrs. Crump announced. "Please take out a piece of paper." Noticing no response from Todd, she asked. "Todd, are you all right?" Slowly he raised his head and looked at the teacher. Snickers could be heard from classmates. "Please get ready for your spelling test," Mrs. Crump continued, ignoring the suppressed laughter.

When the class was over, Dave made his way toward Todd. He was busy gathering his papers and books together. "Todd," Dave interrupted. "I don't know if you collect baseball cards, but I had this extra one you can have."

Todd took the baseball card and clumsily tucked it in among his books. Without a word of response, he turned to leave. Nevertheless,

Dave walked beside Todd to science class, not uncomfortable with the silence.

* * *

After school, the boys saw Jodi and waved to her as they were boarding the bus. She had been right. The last question on the science test had asked them to explain how the universe came into being. They would have to wait to see how Mr. Carbunkle responded to their answers.

The next day in science class, the test papers were returned to the students. Mr. Carbunkle cleared his throat and crossed his arms over his broad chest. "Let's go over the test questions, so everyone understands why I graded the papers as I did."

The teacher went through each question, giving the correct answer and explaining each one. When he got to the last question, he paused. The tip of his tongue appeared in the corner of his mouth and crossed his lips. He always did this when he was concentrating on something.

"Some of you seem confused about this question, 'How did the universe begin?'" he said. "I thought I made it very clear what the textbook said, but some of you," he paused and looked at Larry, "came up with the old Bible theory that's been proven wrong long ago. Don't you know that the Bible version is a myth? It's impossible for all of this to have happened in six days as the Bible suggests. What made you believe such a crazy idea?" he said as he pointed to Larry.

"Sir," Larry said, "I know it sounds pretty crazy. But to me, it sounds crazier to believe that this whole universe happened on its own after a big explosion. I believe a very intelligent being had to invent and create everything. The stars and planets travel in their orbits without crashing. There are so many different kinds of creatures and plants. That's why I believe there's a God." Larry was surprised how brave he was, and that these words came out of his mouth.

The teacher's face grew red, and his lips clenched together. Jodi raised her hand. Mr. Carbunkle couldn't remember her name, so he pointed at her.

"I feel that since no one was really there when it happened, all of these ideas are only theories anyway. I also choose the Bible version," Jodi said.

Mr. Carbunkle scowled, stroked his chin, and backed against his desk. As he leaned on the desk, his large bottom bumped a flask of fluid that was sitting there. It crashed to the floor, breaking into many pieces. A startled look passed over Mr. Carbunkle's face as he jumped away from the desk. He heard muffled laughter around the classroom. Dave waved his hand.

"Mr. Carbunkle," Dave spoke up, "that glass sure made a big bang. But I don't think if we left it there for a long time, it would ever get fixed all by itself. That's why I believe God made the universe—maybe He did it with a big bang, but He was there fixing things!"

Just then, the bell rang. Class was dismissed, and Mr. Carbunkle began mopping up the mess.

Chapter 15

The Move

When school was out, Larry found Dave and Jodi. "Is anyone interested in taking the bus to my place to look at ORB?" Larry asked.

"*Yes,*" Jodi said emphatically. "I think science class might be quite interesting!"

"I think so too," Larry returned. "And I need help answering that message in the bottle we found at the beach."

"And maybe my grandparents have sent me a message," Dave added as they boarded the bus and sat down.

"Oh my god," Jodi gasped. Larry and Dave followed her gaze. Just outside the bus window, a group of students were gathering around a fight. In the center of the group were Todd and another boy, pounding each other with their fists. Todd's nose was bleeding. The taller boy, Josh, had the advantage with longer arms and bigger muscles. But Todd's anger spurred him on like a mad man. The students started taking sides, mostly for Josh. They shouted and cheered when Josh got in a good punch. Todd refused to quit. He now had a cut over his eyebrow. At last two teachers emerged from the school and broke up the fight.

"Todd has a hard time," Dave commented quietly.

When the friends arrived at his house, Larry led the way to his room and opened the door. Tiger was sprawled across the desk.

"Hey you," Larry complained to the cat. "This is my desk you know, but I'll share my bed with you." He scooped the cat in his arms and laid him on the bed. The cat opened his eyes sleepily, stretched, and went back to sleep. "Lazy cat!" Larry muttered.

"What's this box on your desk that Tiger was sleeping on?" Jodi picked up a small flat green box with ribbon. "Are you having another birthday?"

"I have no idea what that is." Larry was puzzled. "Open it."

Jodi untied the ribbon and lifted the lid. Inside were three small silver pieces. The friends laughed with glee. "Pieces for our k-suns," they chorused together.

"Our angels do like to have fun, don't they?" Larry observed as they each pulled their k-suns out to look at them. "So which piece goes to whom?" It took a few minutes to unscramble the puzzle.

When the pieces were snapped into place, Larry opened his desk and found ORB. "See this clever bag that Jodi found to keep ORB in?"

Dave and Jodi watched as Larry unzipped the black bag. "It really works well. It fits perfectly! And it keeps the light in," they commented.

"Who wants to go first?" Larry asked.

"Ladies, first," Dave suggested. Larry agreed and handed ORB to Jodi. She was getting used to their special treatment of her, so she accepted ORB without argument. There was J-gette, greeting her with a smile. "You kids did well in science class today. You honored Good One. He loves you so much. Hope you like the new pieces for your k-suns."

"We do. You make it so much fun!" Jodi giggled. Then she pushed the RW button and began to watch science class. "Interesting, interesting," she kept repeating. "L-mor was really helping you with words, Larry. And J-gette was really happy with the way we stood up for the Good One. And," she paused and broke into a laugh. "Poor, Mr. Carbunkle! You should see the funny expression on the evil angel's face when the glass broke. He was not happy!"

The smile left Jodi's face as she began watching the next scene, the fist fight. As the fight began and Jodi had gasped, "Oh my god," she saw her angel's reaction. J-gette shook her head and covered her face and ears. Even though Jodi could see the good and evil angels involved actively with the fight, it was J-gette's reaction to her words that puzzled her.

"Tell me what's wrong," Jodi pleaded.

"Oh, it's the careless use of the word 'God' that hurts our ears," J-gette said with tears in her eyes. "Hesperus has a legion called 'Insults.' They encourage humans to use God's name carelessly. It is used without respect for who he is or for his feelings. After all he has done to rescue humans and then to have his name used with no thought of him is hurtful to him. It hurts us who follow him, too."

"I didn't even realize what I was doing," Jodi said regretfully. "I'm sorry, please forgive me. I'll pay more attention to what I say. I want to be on the Good One's side—not on his enemy's side."

J-gette smiled through her tears and hugged Jodi. "I know you do, and I knew you'd understand someday."

Jodi was thoughtful as she handed ORB to Dave. "Thanks," Dave said. "I want to talk to D-go about Todd." He pushed the RW button and watched the morning's scene in homeroom replay when Dave gave the baseball card to Todd. There were many evil angels surrounding Todd, and the webs were wrapped around him so tightly, he could hardly function emotionally. Angels from Leo's revenge gang were there, along with angels from the gangs of Self-pity, Devaluation, Blaming, and Killing. He saw how an evil angel tried to block Dave's words so that Todd was barely aware he was there. D-go tried to move the evil angel out of the way, but he resisted D-go, repeating the words, "He's chosen me. He's chosen me!"

When the scene was over, Dave asked D-go about Todd. "Is there something we can do to help free Todd for the Good One's kingdom?" he asked.

"I'm proud of you!" D-go said with a pat on Dave's back. "Keep trying to get Todd's attention. Your words are louder to him than mine or his angel, right now. His angel is really discouraged, but he will help as much as he is given permission to. The baseball card is a good idea."

Then Dave noticed Larry looking at his e-mails. "You'll want to go see your e-mail, now," D-go pointed to the computer. He waved and said, "It's been nice talking to you!"

"Here's an e-mail from your grandparents," Larry motioned Dave to the computer. Dave leaned over and read the words eagerly:

Dear Dave,

We had a safe trip home. We are excited to be moving back to Warrenville, and have begun packing things in boxes. The old home has many memories for me of my grandparents, and stories my father told me of his childhood. We'll have to share them sometime. And of course, we are excited to be moving closer to you. It will be fun to get better acquainted. We've taken your laptop to the computer doctor, and hopefully it will soon be as good as new. We send our love,

Grandpa and Grandma Warren.

It took awhile for Dave to think of how to answer the e-mail. His life didn't seem that exciting, except for ORB and the discoveries there. Of course, he couldn't talk about that. He sat down and wrote:

Dear Grandma and Grandpa,

Things are about the same here. We had a science test yesterday and I passed. After school I hang out with my friends. I haven't told Dad about you yet. I miss you, and can hardly wait till you move here.

Love, Dave

While Dave was working on his e-mail, Larry and Jodi began looking at the message that they had found in the bottle at the beach:

Help me find God. I want to be happy.
Angelina Cortez, age 12, #32 Blanco Road, Manila, Philippines

"What should I say?" Larry wondered.
"Why don't you ask L-mor?" Jodi suggested.

"Of course," Larry said sheepishly. "Why didn't I think of that?" He put ORB to his eyes, and smiled as he found L-mor right by his side.

"I heard that," L-mor joked. "Why don't you tell her about the Oracles? She will have access to a copy in the Philippines."

"Great!" Larry said. "Is there anything else you need to tell me while I can hear you?"

"Just that we, the Good One's family, are very proud of the way you defended our cause in science class today. You were really in tune with us. It took courage to do what you did. As for the future, join Dave in helping us with Todd. We are losing him to Hesperus's side. And your sister—she's a very special person even though she annoys you at times. Help her learn more about us."

"Thanks," Larry responded. "We will. And thanks for the surprise box. I liked that!" He put ORB gently in its case and bag, and then picked up a paper and pencil.

Dear Angelina,

My friend and I found the bottle you sent with a message. It came ashore on Paradise Beach in Oregon, USA. We were surprised that it had come thousands of miles across the ocean, from your country to ours. It took about two years to get here.

We are also trying to know God better. We are reading about him in the Holy Bible. It is helping us find happiness. Perhaps you have a Bible to read?

I am fifteen years old and live with my parents. I have one sister and good friends Dave and Jodi. Please tell us more about your life in the Philippines. Do you have a computer and an e-mail address?

Larry Foster, age fifteen
441 SW 4th Street, Warrenville, Oregon, USA
E-mail address: LarryF@yahoo.com

* * *

The next few weeks sped by. The boys learned more about Todd. He was an only child, and like Dave, lived with his father. They lived in an isolated wooded area in the country, so it made it harder to do things with him after school. But they found ways to talk to Todd at school, and tried to include him in their group. However, Todd held back, reluctant to make friends.

Grandpa and Grandma Warren kept in contact each week. Their moving date was set for December 10, and they were looking forward to their first Christmas with Dave. He could hardly wait. When December 10 arrived, Dave and Larry made special arrangements to go to the Warrens' home after school, to see if they could help with anything.

Mrs. Warren greeted them with a big hug. "The movers have almost finished unloading the van," she said. "They've got the bed set up, and it's made. Now I'm just unloading the kitchen boxes. It would help if you would flatten the empty boxes and put them in a stack on the front porch."

The boys were eager to help, and when that job was finished, they found tasks to do for Grandpa Warren. "I've got something to give you, Dave," Grandpa said, smiling. "Here's a cell phone for you. Now you can call us anytime you want—we're on a family plan."

Dave's eyes grew big and then misted. "Thank you, Grandpa. You make me feel so much safer." Grandpa smiled and hugged Dave.

"And now, I want to show you around this old house. It has quite a history. My father tells me there used to be a secret passage in the house somewhere. His mother was a sickly lady, and the servants could use the secret passage to go directly to her room to take care of her. But I have no idea if the passage still exists." He led them up the oak staircase. It turned and opened into a short but wide hall. There were three large bedrooms, a bathroom, and another narrower staircase leading to the attic. "The last time I looked in the attic, there were still treasures there from previous owners. You might have fun poking around in the chests and boxes."

The boys glanced at each other with knowing looks. "That would sure be fun," Dave said. Grandpa led them back down the stairs. On the main floor, there was another bedroom, a bathroom, an office, a large living room, and dining room. There were two fireplaces. The whole house was trimmed in oak wood with oak beams crossing the living room ceiling. There were built-in cupboards, window seats, and cubby holes. The bay window looked onto the yard. "When I was a little tyke," Grandpa reminisced, "I used to love playing hide-and-seek at this house when we came to visit my grandparents.

There are so many places to hide in these cubby holes and window boxes."

Grandma was still in the kitchen, filling the pantry with the contents of more boxes. "We'll be back to help you flatten more boxes, just as soon as Grandpa is finished showing us around," Dave said.

"Take your time," Grandma chuckled. "This old house has lots of nooks and crannies to explore."

Grandpa led the boys down another flight of stairs. "This basement used to be the living quarters for the servants. This open area was used as a workroom to do the laundry, the mending, or preparing foods for the winter. The smaller rooms around are where the servants slept."

"Wow, this is a cool house," Dave said. "Do you think the secret passage started down here then?"

"It could have, or it might have been in the kitchen area or pantry," Grandpa replied. "It would be fun to find it, wouldn't it?"

The boys nodded.

"We have something fun to look forward to, then!" Grandpa smiled.

Chapter 16

Christmas Together

The weather was crispy cold, and the days shorter. But Christmas lights decorated houses and yards in Warrenville, making the darkness cheery and festive. Storefronts were filled with tempting gift ideas to place under trees. People were bustling around with purpose, preparing for the holiday season. The students at school had put on an outstanding Christmas program.

Dave still had not told his father that Grandpa and Grandma Warren had moved to town. He was building his courage for just the right moment. Now the Foster family was inviting him and his father, along with the Warrens, for Christmas dinner. It would be the perfect time to tell him. He would have a lot of good support.

Mr. Foster set up the Christmas tree and put on the lights. The rest of the family finished decorating the tree, and with each passing day, more gifts appeared beneath it. The excitement was building, with secrets, good smells, and fun music.

Larry and Dave used ORB as often as possible, and their angels had explained the meaning of Christmas. They encouraged the youths to read the first Christmas story, found in the Bible. What a wonderful story of Jesus, the Good One's son, coming to earth in human form to live with humans. He was disguised as a newborn baby and raised by human parents. It was almost like a secret mission, with very few people understanding who he was until the right time, just as the Good One had planned.

Larry wondered how he could help the family understand the real meaning of Christmas. Then one day as he and Dave were walking past the Hallmark store, they spotted something in the window. "Look!" Larry said, pointing with excitement to a little arrangement of figurines. "It's a miniature stable with baby Jesus lying in the manger. There's his mother and father."

"And there are the shepherds and wise men!" Dave added.

"I wonder how much it costs," Larry leaned closer to the window to have a better look.

"Let's go find out," Dave suggested.

The boys looked dejected when they discovered the price: $49.99. That was more than either of them had, even if they put their money together.

But the next day, Dave was excited to tell Larry something. "Grandpa Warren has a job for us to do. The leaves never got raked in his yard this fall, and he'll pay us to do it!"

"That's super! It'll be a cold job, but it's worth it," Larry replied, clapping his friend on the back.

The next day, Larry came home with a big sack. "Mom," he called as he entered the door. "I have something for you! Actually, it's something for the whole family, but I thought you should be in charge of it," Larry handed the sack to his mother.

"How lovely!" Mrs. Foster lifted the box to her lap and looked at the picture on the box. "What made you think of this?"

"Dave and I wanted us all to remember the story of the very first Christmas," Larry said thoughtfully. "We thought this would help."

Mrs. Foster smiled. "Well, this will sure do that. Let's see where we should set it up." She walked into the living room. "What do you think about on the coffee table? Will Tiger leave it alone if we put it there?"

Larry smiled when he thought of his cat. Tiger always had to smell everything new that came into the house. "We'll make sure he behaves himself," Larry chuckled. "I think the coffee table would be the perfect place."

Mrs. Foster opened the box, and the two of them began arranging the miniature stable and the figures of baby Jesus, his mother, father, the shepherds, and others. "I had forgotten about the Christmas story," she said as she admired the figurines. "I'm so glad you are reminding us."

Just then Tiger paraded into the room, his nose held high and his nostrils quivering as he sniffed the air to detect where the new smell was coming from. He sat nearby, sniffing, and watching Mrs. Foster and Larry arranging the scene. Then he noticed the empty box. Immediately, he hopped in and curled up comfortably. Larry piled the wadded up wrapping paper on top of the cat, and he was content to stay where he was. Larry moved the box under the Christmas tree. Tiger still remained in the box.

"It's a good place to leave him," Mrs. Foster smiled. "He will stay out of mischief for a while."

Christmas day arrived at last. A few snowflakes were falling, something unusual for this part of Oregon. It made the day even more special. Mrs. Foster had the turkey roasting in the oven, and the air was full of good smells. Excitement built as the guests began to arrive. The Warrens came with arms full of gifts. Dave and his dad arrived a bit later, Mr. Lister walking unsteadily. He seemed to be in a good mood, talking loudly and laughing frequently.

"Merry Christmas," he roared, "and Happy New Year!" The greeting seemed a bit insincere to folk, but they accepted his words graciously. "Same to you," they responded. When the introductions were made, it took a few moments for Mr. Lister to realize who the Warrens were. He became subdued and thoughtful.

Mr. Warren extended his hand warmly. "It's been a long time, David. We hope you don't mind us connecting with the family again. We wanted to see our grandson. We are sorry for all the hurt feelings and sadness our family has experienced. We hope we can see each other more often."

Mr. Lister looked at the faces around him and hesitated. He took Mr. Warren's hand and shook it briefly. There were too many people here to make a scene. His foggy mind was spinning. He'd deal with it later. He wished he could have another drink. He excused himself to the bathroom. There he could take a little sip of the comforting fluid from the flask he had tucked inside his jacket pocket.

"Gift time," Mr. Foster announced. "Let's gather in the living room, everyone." He gave Dave and Larry each a Santa hat and asked them to distribute the gifts one at a time.

In about an hour, the gifts had all been opened. People were inspecting their new gifts and sharing comments about them. Grandpa and Grandma Warren had given Dave and his dad matching shirts, Mr. and Mrs. Foster were talking about the new DVD series they had received, Larry had some new games to try, and Cheryl was holding a new sweater up to her face and looking at herself in the mirror.

Mrs. Foster excused herself to finish the dinner preparations. Before long, she was inviting everyone to the table. It was beautiful, with a Christmas tablecloth, glowing candles, and lots of good food. As they gathered in their places, Mr. Warren made a request. "This is such a special time for us, I'd like to pause and thank the good Lord for this happy occasion."

"That's fine," Mrs. Foster agreed, not knowing what else to say. The Fosters were not used to praying at their house, but everyone sensed that something special was about to happen. Silence came over the group as Mr. Warren bowed his head and began talking to God as if he were a friend. The words came from his thankful heart. When he said "Amen," there was silence for a moment, and then conversation slowly began again.

Soon everyone was heaping their plates with food. Mr. Warren turned to Dave's dad. "So David, what are you doing these days?"

Mr. Lister looked uncomfortable and struggled for words. "I've had a hard time ever since the boy's mother died," his voice slurred. "I couldn't make a living in the building field I'd been trained in. So I've tried first one thing and then another." He paused again and searched for words. "I managed to get a job here at the local bar and grill . . . and that keeps a roof over our heads and food on the table." Mr. Lister squirmed in his seat and looked agitated. He excused himself for a moment. When he returned, there was the smell of fresh alcohol on his breath.

Grandpa Warren remembered David's wedding that warm California summer day. He was marrying their lovely daughter Mary. David was such a promising young man. The two had met at college and courted for several years while David finished his industrial arts degree. David's father was a building contractor, and David was to take over his father's business. Life seemed good for the young couple. Little Davie was born. They had moved into a new house that David had built. And Mary was running a day-care center from their home. Then, the fateful Christmas a few years later, the car accident happened, snuffing out the life of Mary. David was in the hospital unconscious for a week. Fortunately, little Davie had escaped the terrible accident because he had been staying with his grandparents.

When David Lister recovered from the accident, he became very depressed. He was angry at himself as the driver of the car in the accident. He was angry at the Warrens for inviting them to their place for Christmas. The accident would never have happened if they had stayed home. He was angry that he was left with the job of caring for a little boy all by himself. In his depression, he turned to alcohol. His life continued to go downhill. His job and family relationships were ruined. He ran away with Davie, cutting all ties with his former life and leaving no forwarding address.

Grandpa Warren roused himself from the past. Putting on a cheerful voice, he said, "Well, today is our first Christmas in Warrenville. We hope to have many more here. Next Christmas, we can all come to our house. We should be nicely settled by then. By the way, I must give you all our new business card with our address and phone number."

David Lister excused himself early from the Christmas gathering. He and Dave disappeared out the door and into the snow alone.

* * *

Later that evening, the phone rang. Grandpa Warren looked at his watch. It was 9:00 p.m.

"Mr. Warren, this is Officer Wright from the Warrenville police," spoke the voice from the phone. "We have an unidentified young man here at the hospital. Because of his injuries, we are not able to talk to him. We found your business card in his pocket, and thought you might know who he is. Would you please come to the Emergency Department at the hospital?"

Grandpa Warren instantly remembered the recent trip with Dave to the hospital Emergency Department, and fear welled up inside him. There was a lump in his throat as he replied, "Yes, of course, of course. We'll be right there."

Chapter 17

The New Home

Mr. and Mrs. Warren stepped into the waiting room of the hospital emergency room. In one corner sat a mother comforting her bawling baby. A few chairs down sat an old man, his head in his hands. Two grown children were on either side of him, trying to comfort him.

Mr. Warren stepped up to the receptionist's desk. A young lady dressed in green scrubs greeted them. "I'm Mr. Warren. Officer Wright called me about fifteen minutes ago," Mr. Warren began.

"Yes, just a moment," the young lady replied.

A minute later, Officer Wright greeted them, and led them to an exam room. Their worst nightmare had come true. It was hard to recognize Dave. He looked so lifeless on the gurney. His body was wrapped in layers of blankets. There was a big bruise over one eye, and a bandage covering a head wound. He was connected to a beeping monitor at the head of the bed. A nurse was examining Dave's eyes by lifting his eyelids and looking at his pupils.

Tears came to Mrs. Warren's eyes, and her hand instinctively went to her mouth to cover a gasp. Mr. Warren put his arm around his wife to comfort her.

"It is our grandson, Dave Lister," Mr. Warren told the officer. His voice seemed to catch in his throat.

A look of recognition came to Officer Wright's face. "Oh, this is David Lister's boy. We had him in here a couple of months ago because of abuse issues, didn't we?"

Mr. Warren nodded. "Where did you find him?"

"We found him lying unconscious on the sidewalk along Third Street at 8:05 p.m.," answered the officer. "I brought him straight to the hospital. We found your card in his pocket. That's when I called you. When did you last see him?" the officer questioned.

"We were all together at a Christmas party today at the Fosters' home on Oak Street," Mrs. Warren explained. "Dave and his father left there about 6:00 p.m., planning to walk home. We left an hour or two later."

"What was Mr. Lister's condition when you last saw him?" Officer Wright asked.

"We could tell he had been drinking. He was a bit wobbly on his feet. He must have brought his own supply of booze because the Fosters did not serve any alcoholic drinks at the party." Mrs. Warren paused. "Today was the first time Mr. Lister has seen us in about ten years. After our daughter's death, he became depressed and disappeared with the boy. It was the boy that found us through the Internet a couple of months ago. Mr. Lister may have been upset today when he learned that we are back in the boy's life. But we didn't have much indication that he was upset at seeing us."

"Is the boy going to be all right?" Mrs. Warren raised her eyebrows. Concern was written in her eyes. She leaned over Dave and spoke softly in his ear. "Grandma and Grandpa are with you now, Dave. Everything's going to be okay. We love you." There was no response from Dave, except for a raise in the heartbeat on the monitor.

"I'll let the doctor know you are here," Officer Wright said. "He can tell you about the boy's condition. In the meantime, I will pay a visit to Mr. Lister, and see what he has to say about this. He is the one who is strongly suspected of hurting the boy. It would be helpful if the boy could tell us himself, but that is not possible at this time."

"Before you go," Mr. Warren interjected, "What are the chances of being awarded the legal guardianship for Dave? I've been very worried about the young man's safety ever since the last incident. Now I wish we had taken action sooner."

"Your chances are good," the officer replied. "We'll make a copy of the paperwork here, and you can set up an appointment with Family Services tomorrow. They will lead you through the hoops."

Officer Wright excused himself, and in a few minutes, the doctor entered the room and introduced himself. His expression was grave. "Your grandson is unconscious and in serious condition. We don't know when he'll wake up. It could be in a few hours, or it could be days. He's been injured pretty badly. He's suffering from exposure. His temperature is below normal, so we are taking steps to get it back up. His heartbeat is strong, so that is in his favor. We will also be doing some x-rays shortly to see the extent of his injuries. With open wounds like he's received, there is chance of infection. But we will be admitting him to the intensive care unit soon, so he can receive the best care and be monitored closely."

Two orderlies appeared at the door ready to transport Dave to his hospital room. "You may come with us," one of them said to Mr. and Mrs. Warren. As the little procession worked its way through the halls, Mr. Warren turned to his wife, "I think one of us should stay with Dave until he wakes up." She nodded in agreement. He continued, "You should go home and get some rest. I'll take the first shift."

* * *

Mrs. Warren arrived at the hospital just after 8:00 a.m. the next morning. "How is he?" she anxiously asked her weary husband.

"He seems about the same," Mr. Warren replied. "However, his temperature is back up to normal, and the nurse seems to think that his sleep isn't as deep as it was at first. That's a sign that he's recovering."

"That's good." Mrs. Warren sounded hopeful. "I called the Fosters to let them know what happened. Now, why don't you go get a bite of breakfast before you go home to get some sleep?"

"Okay," Mr. Warren yawned. "But I want to stop by Family Services first to start the process for us to be foster parents."

"That's good," Mrs. Warren agreed. "Hopefully we'll have good news here by the time you return." Before she settled in the recliner chair beside Dave's bed, she took his hand and stroked it. Softly, she spoke to him. "Dave, Grandma is here with you now. We want you to get well soon." She felt him gently squeeze her hand in response. "Thank God!" she whispered.

Just after lunch, Mrs. Foster, Larry, and Cheryl came to the hospital. One at a time they spent a few minutes in Dave's room. Mrs. Warren suggested that each of them talk to Dave to encourage him, even if it appeared he didn't hear them.

Larry moved close to the bed. "Hey, my buddy, this is Larry," he said. "You've been hurt badly, but we're just waiting for you to wake up! Jodi told me to tell you to get well soon. We all miss you." Dave's eyelids twitched, then relaxed.

"These little signs are encouraging," Mrs. Warren said with a slight smile. "This morning he squeezed my hand when I spoke to him."

When Cheryl saw Dave's patched-up head, she was touched with sympathy. She moved closer to his face. "Dave, this is Cheryl. We sure want you to get well soon." She fastened a colorful Mylar balloon to the foot of his bed.

Officer Wright visited the hospital in the late afternoon. "How is the patient?" he asked.

"He's still not awake, but we see little signs that he is improving," Mrs. Warren answered.

"You'll be interested to know that Mr. Lister has been arrested and is in jail," said the officer. "We will still need Dave's story when he wakes up, but at least he will be safe from his father."

Mrs. Warren nodded, "We're glad to hear that."

In parting, Officer Wright assured the family that he would keep in touch.

It wasn't long before Mr. Warren returned. He looked refreshed and encouraged. "We will be able to take Dave to our house when he is discharged from the hospital," he smiled.

"That's wonderful, dear," Mrs. Warren looked relieved. "Why don't you tell him?"

Mr. Warren stepped to Dave's side and took his hand. "Dave, this is Grandpa Warren. You'll be coming home with us just as soon as you get out of here. So hurry and get well!"

Dave's fingers squeezed his grandpa's hand. His eyes fluttered and opened with a vacant stare.

"It's nice to see your eyes open," Grandpa smiled. "I think you are waking up." But Dave's eyes closed again.

Just then the nurse came to check on her patient. "It looks like he is slowly rousing," she said, "but we won't know until he is fully awake to assess if there is permanent brain damage." Mr. and Mrs. Warren were sober. Even though they were hopeful, they knew that Dave's condition was still very serious.

It wasn't until the next day that Dave woke up enough to recognize people and to make sense when he talked. What a day of rejoicing that was! Every day after that, he improved more and more, until at last, he could eat by himself and walk by himself.

"I think you can go home in the morning," the doctor announced one afternoon. "I know a couple of grandparents who are very eager for that to happen." There were smiles all around.

* * *

Grandma Warren helped Dave up the oak stairs in his new home. "We've prepared the front corner room for you. We hope you like it. We bought a few things for you to use until you are well enough to stop by your dad's house to pick up your own things."

"Grandma thinks of everything," Dave thought.

Grandma opened the door to his new room. Dave could hardly believe his eyes. The room was large and sunny. There were twin beds with matching bedspreads and a computer desk with his laptop in the center. It had been repaired and looked as good as new. A chest of drawers and a closet were already stocked with clothes. A small bookcase with a few books stood in one corner, and lamps on nightstands made it look comfortable and inviting.

"Oh, thank you!" Dave exclaimed. "It's wonderful." He walked slowly to the window to take in the view. Down the street, he could see the park where old Open-Mouth tree looked over the baseball diamond. The other window looked into the yard. A row of evergreen trees stood not far from the house.

Grandma sat down in a chair to rest. Just then, Grandpa entered the room. "So you like it," he smiled as he set down a few bags they had brought from the hospital. "I think my grandma liked it too. This was her room."

"You mean this was the room where the secret passage came?" Dave asked.

Grandpa nodded. “Maybe if you stay here awhile, you’ll be able to solve the mystery!” A smile crept over Dave’s face.

“Now,” said Grandma with a smile, “before you solve the mystery, we need to get this young man well! I’ll bring up a bite of lunch for Dave in a few minutes, and then he needs to rest.”

Chapter 18

Angel Athletes

The next day, while Dave was resting in his new room, there was a knock at the door. "It's your buddy Larry, coming to hassle you!" Larry announced.

"Come in," Dave called eagerly. "It's good to see you!"

"This is cool," Larry was enthusiastic as he looked around Dave's comfortable new room. "You can even have a sleepover if you want. You have two beds."

"This is the room where the secret passage might have ended," Dave said in a mysterious voice. "This was my great-great-grandmother's room."

"You're serious?" Larry questioned. Dave nodded with a sparkle in his eye.

"Have you tried to find it yet?" Larry asked.

"Not yet!" Dave replied. "And I haven't explored the attic either. Grandma wants me to stay close to my bed."

"I'm sure she knows best," Larry chuckled. "But before you know it, you'll be well enough to explore every inch of this old house!" He looked out first one window and then the next. "You can see the park from here!" he observed, and then turned to the closet door. "Is this whole wall a closet? It sure is long."

Dave opened the closet and looked inside. It was long. There were built-in shelves on either end. "They look pretty solid," he mused. "Can you see anything that looks like it slides or swings out?"

Larry examined the shelves closely. "Not really, but the shelves at this end are different from the ones at the other end."

"So they are," Dave nodded. He noticed that one side was built with dark oak wood, and the other side with slightly lighter wood. "I wonder if someone built these later and closed up the secret passage. Sometime I'll ask Grandpa to look at it, and see what he thinks. Another idea is the floor. I wonder what's hidden under the carpet."

It was intriguing to think about the possibilities of where a passage could be hidden. The floor was not completely carpeted. There was a border of hardwood flooring all around the edge of the carpet. Dave tried lifting the carpet. It came up on the edge. "We'd have to move all the furniture to see underneath the whole thing." Larry said. "We need to wait till you're feeling stronger."

"Probably a good idea," Dave agreed with a sigh.

* * *

Within a few days, Dave was well enough to get his belongings from his old home. When Grandpa drove up to the forlorn little house, a sob caught in Dave's throat. So much sadness and fear had taken place here. With his dad in jail, there was no worry about his safety. Yet, there was a longing in his heart that Dad would be kind and caring like his grandparents were. He put the longing thoughts behind him, and was glad for the big improvement his life had taken over the past few weeks.

Dave collected his clothes from his old room and pulled the big family Bible from where it was hidden beneath the bed. This was a true treasure for him. He wanted to keep it with him forever. He also went to the bookshelf and took the picture of his mother, his Little League trophy, and the glass ball with the miniature snow-covered village. He turned it upside down and smiled as he watched the snow floating down on the village. He would take that, too. When they had finished collecting the things and closed the door behind them, a chapter in Dave's life also closed.

"Let's stop by your friend Larry's house," Grandpa suggested. "Maybe he'd like to come for another visit."

It didn't take long for Larry to pull on his coat. Christmas vacation had seemed long and uninteresting without his best friend to do things with. He was glad to see Dave out of bed and recovering so well from the injuries of Christmas day. "Tell Mom I'm over at Dave's," Larry shouted to his sister Cheryl.

Larry helped Dave and his grandparents unpack the things they had brought from Dave's old home. When everything was in place, the grandparents excused themselves so the young men could be alone.

Larry reached in his pocket. "I brought ORB," he said. "You haven't had a chance to talk to D-go for a while. I thought you might enjoy that."

"Oh yes," Dave agreed. He pulled ORB's case from the bag and opened it.

"Well, well!" D-go greeted him. "It's been so long since we've talked. You've had a very hectic time since Christmas! Things are working out much better for you, aren't they?"

Dave grinned, "They sure are."

"Well, you've kept me pretty busy, too, I must say. But the evil angels had a bitter-sweet victory. They've got your dad where they want him, but they're not happy that things are going so well for you. Guerdon's team has been working for many months to get everything arranged for you. It took Hesperus and his angels by surprise!" D-go smiled.

"It's truly a miracle how everything worked out," Dave marveled. "And for Grandpa to be able to buy this house that his dad grew up in is so amazing."

D-go smiled broadly. "That was a fun gift to bring about. And because of it, I have something for your k-sun." He held out a large silver piece.

"Wow!" Dave exclaimed. "This one is so big it covers all the bars." He snapped the piece into place. What had once looked like a miniature prison with bars was now covered with silver siding. The k-sun was transformed into a little house, looking very much like a picture of Dave's new home.

D-go looked pleased as he watched Dave admire the new look. "You've been rescued from your prison, so to speak. Your prison has been changed into a home. It represents your new freedom!"

"I'm so happy," Dave murmured.

"I also have something else that you and your friends might be interested in," D-go continued. "Tomorrow afternoon, half of Good

One's angels are holding a game event. We compete in different games and races, just to try out our skills and take a break from all the serious work we do."

"That sounds like fun," Dave replied. "Why do only half of them get to come to the games?"

"Someone has to take care of Good One's business," D-go smiled. "So we take turns having time off. Meet me in the gazebo behind your house tomorrow afternoon. Invite Larry and his sister and Jodi if you want. I think you will enjoy yourselves."

* * *

The next afternoon, the friends were in high spirits as they bundled Dave up for the adventure in the Warren's backyard. It was a large yard that was surrounded by the winter forest. The grass still held hints of green, but it was mixed with the brown blades of winter. The forest held a few evergreen trees, but the rest had dropped their leaves. Their naked gray trunks and branches looked stark against the cloudy sky. The gazebo was near the back of the yard, with landscaping that gave it the appearance of blending into the forest. The flowerbeds that surrounded it were mostly bare, but contained a few wilted remains of plants.

From inside the house, the Warrens watched the young people who were obviously enjoying each other's company. It puzzled them that they would want to be outside in the cold when there was a nice warm house to use. Nevertheless, it was good that the kids were at their place. They were happy to see that the friends were treating Dave with extra care. They were still fussing over him with his recovery from head injuries.

The four young people sat down on the benches inside the gazebo. Larry pulled ORB's case from his pocket, and offered the glasses to his friends. "Let's draw straws to see who goes first," he said playfully.

"Just don't cheat," Cheryl bantered as a sibling will do.

Larry ignored her comment and replied, "Cheryl, please prepare the straws then." She shrugged and picked up a twig and broke it into four different lengths.

"Whoever gets the long straw goes first," she said. Cheryl turned her back to the group and arranged the twigs carefully in her hand.

When she turned back to the group, only the tops of the twigs could be seen in her hand. One by one, the young people chose a twig. "It's Jodi who goes first," announced Cheryl when they had all compared the twigs.

Jodi was happy to be first. "What a lucky break!" she exclaimed. "It's been such a long time since I've talked to J-gette!" She lifted ORB to her eyes and smiled broadly as J-gette greeted her.

"The event will begin soon," J-gette said. "We're just waiting for everyone to arrive. In the meantime, let me tell you that no matter which twig you drew, it was the right one! Here's your twig, and yours and yours!" She touched Cheryl's eyes, then Larry's and Dave's. Immediately they could all see in the fifth dimension. Cheryl had not had much experience with ORB or the wonderful fifth dimension world, but she recognized her angel C-tel.

The first thing the young people noticed was that it was no longer winter! Their coats and scarves had disappeared. The trees were clothed in vibrant new leaves. The grass was spring green. Flowers were blooming in the beds, and the smell from fragrant blossoms filled the warm air. The sun was shining, and the sky was blue. "It's forever spring when we have these events," J-gette called in glee, her arms stretched outward and upward.

"Everyone has arrived now except Guerdon," L-mor explained. "He comes to open the games."

The young people looked at thousands and thousands of shining angels that were gathered for the event. There was no auditorium or seats for them to sit on, yet the angels balanced themselves in the air in such a way that they appeared in organized tiers around the central open area. Suddenly it grew darker and darker, and then, it was as if a lightning bolt descended into that open area. A dazzling creature appeared, so bright there was no need for a spotlight. A golden crown was on his head. As he raised his left hand, a golden pillar grew magically from the ground. It grew and grew until it was as tall as the imaginary auditorium they had filled. "We are the light of the world," shouted Guerdon as he flew to the top of the pillar and touched it with his right hand. Immediately, the top of the pole flashed with fireworks greater than the world had ever seen. Patterns of beautiful light and colors shot from the pole for several minutes, and then the light and sparks were drawn back to the pole until they rested on top continuing to hiss and dance like a giant sparkler.

"May the games begin, my faithful ones!" Guerdon shouted as he mysteriously disappeared. Instantly, the darkness was gone. The light returned.

A powerful angel stepped to the center of the group. "Our first game is a simple one. It is called *Seek the Lost.* You have already formed two teams. One team will be the *Lost* team. You will be hiding by exhibiting your skills at costuming. You may create any costume with which you desire to disguise yourself. The only thing you cannot disguise is the red heart you wear on your forehead. It must still be visible somewhere on your new costume. The other team will be the *Seekers.* As soon as you have found a *Lost* comrade, bring him or her here to the center of the arena. While I am counting, the seekers must close their eyes. At the count of ten, those on the *Lost* team should be hiding in your new costumes, and the *Seekers* may begin."

"We've got to join our teams now," D-go called to the kids as he flew away. "See if you can find us!"

When the leading angel began counting, there was a flurry of excitement that subsided into stillness. At the count of ten, the *Seekers* began their search. They looked for those red hearts that would be shining somewhere on anything the *Lost* comrade may have chosen to become, perhaps a bird, a squirrel, a tree, a flower, or a rock.

Just then, a cat that looked like Tiger rubbed against Larry's leg. "Tiger!" Larry exclaimed without thinking. "How did you get here?" It was then he noticed the faint red heart waving at the end of his tail. A golden angel flew up and scooped the cat in his arms. "Very clever, L-mor, but I found you!" said the angel as he carried the cat to the center of the circle.

A robin hopped onto the railing of the gazebo. It winked at Jodi, and then flew away. "Did I see a red heart on the robin's breast?" she questioned. "It happened so fast!"

Before long, the center of the circle was filled with all types of animals, birds, moving trees and flowers, and rolling stones. There were sounds of amusement as *Seeker* angels chuckled and commented on the variety of costumes that were exhibited. When everyone had assembled, the leading angel called out, "As you were!" Suddenly all angels were back to their normal shapes and sizes and back in their positions in the imaginary auditorium.

"The next game will be a bit more complicated," the lead angel announced. He waved his hands over the center area. Immediately, beeps sounded as pillars and cross pieces formed one by one into a maze of halls and tunnels. One of the halls was decorated with a chain of orange arrowheads, another with green arrowheads, and another with brown arrowheads. Others had no arrowheads at all. "You all know what the colored arrowheads symbolize," the angel said. "You must avoid flying in those places, and anyone that goes there must drop out of the game. You will all be given golden rackets, and here is the golden ball you will be hitting back and forth to your teammates. You cannot carry the ball or let it drop to the ground. You will be timed. The team that keeps the ball the longest is the winner. There is no need to have rules for fouls since you are on the Good One's side and play with honesty. The team called "Helpers" will come forward now and attach a red belt around your waists. The team called "Mentors" will wear no belts, and they will begin at the signal."

An angel appeared with large cymbals. She brought the shining metal circles together with a resounding crash, and the game began. L-mor, D-go, J-gette, and C-tel were on the Mentor's team together with other angels. They flew through the corridors and windows, swooping up the golden ball with their rackets and tossing it high in the air. Occasionally, the ball would come down in the danger zone, and an angel would sacrifice himself or herself by flying into the forbidden area and rescuing the ball for their team. The game was not only fun, but it took a lot of agility and teamwork to pass the ball to one another in such a complicated maze. They turned, twisted, flew forward or backward through the air. Larry, Dave, Jodi, and Cheryl were thrilled to watch the skill of the players, and they cheered when their angel's team got the ball and kept it in the air. At last the cymbals signaled that the game was over. The Mentors were the winners, and the Helpers congratulated them for their excellence.

"Our last game is a race," the lead angel announced. He pointed to the structure of pillars and crosspieces. The structure creaked, then twisted and turned to create curves and barriers. The angel continued, "You will race in pairs, one angel from each team. Each will be given a handheld flying saucer. When you point it in the direction you desire, it will propel you that way. It will also give you extra speed when you move the accelerator button. Please line up in pairs at the starting point. When the signal is sounded, the pair in the front begins their race. Enjoy the fun."

The cymbals crashed, and the first pair raced down the course, around, and up and down. Shouts and laughter echoed from the chambers of the maze as the flyers were surprised and challenged. Pair after pair emerged from the finish line, laughing and clapping one another on the back, and commenting on the details of the course. They were obviously having a good time.

About half the players had gone through the course, when the sky darkened. An ominous hush fell over the golden angels. They looked up with dismay. They recognized thousands of evil angels swooping in for an attack. The angel who had been leading the games interrupted the hush. "Assume your battle positions," he shouted. The Good One's angels immediately switched from racing to defending. The flying saucers in their hands became golden swords. The struggle was fierce. The light faded. The sparkler pole went out and was swallowed up in the ground. It grew cold, the trees lost their leaves, the flowers shriveled up, and the grass turned brown.

J-gette flew to Jodi's side. "The games are over. There's no need for you to watch this and be alarmed. We will defeat them. Go back inside now." She touched the young people's eyes, and the scene was gone. Jodi removed ORB and gave the glasses to Larry.

The young people were surprised to see it was raining hard. The lightening was flashing, and the thunder was crashing. A fierce wind was blowing the bare tree branches as though they were blades of grass. "Everyone, come inside quickly," Grandpa's anxious voice could barely be heard above the roar of the wind. "This is a terrible storm!"

Chapter 19

A Changed Heart

It took about an hour for the storm to pass on. The four friends gathered in front of the fireplace at the Warrens' house and played a game. But their heart was not in it. They kept thinking about the awesome angel games they had just witnessed. The abrupt end with the arrival of the evil angels was scary, and the terrible storm seemed to symbolize the struggle that was going on between the forces of good and evil.

Cheryl was specially affected by what she had witnessed that afternoon. This was her first real experience with the fifth-dimension world. There was so much she didn't understand. When Mr. Warren retired to his study, and Mrs. Warren decided to make a batch of cookies, the young people were left alone.

"Tell me, who were those angels in the camouflage suits?" Cheryl asked. Dave explained about the angel Hesperus, who somehow thought he could rule the universe better than the Good One does. His rebellion led to the war in the kingdom of R-dor, and then he and his angels were banished to earth. "We have all felt the struggle between good and evil," Dave explained. "ORB has been so helpful to me, so I could understand why my dad is so mean. He has chosen to follow the evil angels. Good One's team used my angel and other good angels to finally rescue me from my dad. They gave me grandparents that I didn't know I had, and a new home. But the war continues as we saw today. Hesperus wants people to join his side because he knows how much it hurts the heart of the Good One. And he hates the good angels."

Jodi explained how her angel, J-gette, had rescued her from the webs that the evil angel had wrapped around her. "I am so much happier now," Jodi said with feeling. "God has sent his spirit, Zephyr, to be with each of us and help us do right. And in addition to that, he has assigned an angel to each of us to help us make good choices. But the evil angels are powerful, too. You know the creature that opened the games today? His name is Guerdon. He is part of God's family, and he came on a secret mission to this earth a long time ago. He was disguised as a baby and grew up as a human being. You've heard the Christmas story about baby Jesus. His story is written in the Bible, and his teachings are wonderful. He helps us to understand the Good One so much better."

"You learned all this because of ORB?" Cheryl asked in amazement. The rest of the group nodded.

Dave added, "ORB and the Oracles, which is the Bible."

"I feel so sorry that I gave ORB to Winnie that time. Please forgive me." Cheryl's eyes passed from one friend to another, searching for acceptance. "How did you ever get ORB back?"

"That was kind of a miracle, too," a smile played at the corner of Larry's mouth. "You tell her, Jodi."

"I found ORB in the garbage can in the girls' restroom at school, and Larry and Dave found its case at the park in front of Open-Mouth tree. Our angels had warned us that the evil angels would try to get ORB from us. They just used you to do that." Cheryl was serious as she thought about all this. She remembered the angel in the camouflage suit that had coaxed her to take ORB from Larry's room.

Just then, Mr. Warren walked into the room. "Is anyone in the mood to explore the attic? With Dave still recovering from his hospital stay, I'm thinking he might appreciate all of your help. We might uncover a lot of mysteries."

"Yes, yes," eager voices chorused.

"Let me get a flashlight so we can find a light switch," Mr. Warren added as he opened a drawer and picked up a yellow and black flashlight. He led the way upstairs, and then opened the door that led to the attic. There was a narrow staircase with steep steps. They felt the cool air coming from the unheated room at the top of the stairs. Dim light filtered down from somewhere above them, but it was not enough to see well. One by one, each person groped their way up the stairs, touching the steps and the sides of the walls with their hands. At the top, Mr. Warren shone his flashlight along the dark unfinished wood. "Aha," he cried as he found a chain. When he pulled it, a light above the stairs clicked on. He moved aside so others could enter the room.

Mr. Warren moved to the center of the room and pulled the light chain that hung there. The large room looked a bit spooky. It was unfinished, but wooden flooring was there to stand on. Rafters draped with cobwebs formed a peak above them. Along two sides of the room, a network of studs and supporting braces rose upward to the rafters. Behind the braces, the area shrunk into the roofline and seemed dark and dusty. Small dirty windows at each end of the room let in a bit of light.

But the large room was fascinating. Cardboard boxes filled with memories stood in one area. A big brown trunk sat at one end. An antique chair frame with a missing seat sat nearby. A bed with old-fashioned bedsprings and mattress was parked along one side, and a chamber pot was underneath. A rickety chest of drawers was covered with dust. Sheets covered larger pieces of furniture. An old calendar hung from a nail on a stud. A child's rocking chair sat forlornly alone.

"Let's explore," Mr. Warren's voice held a hint of mystery. "I don't know if there's anything left here from my family, but I would love to find more clues about them. Dave, you might want to sit on that old bed and direct the search. We don't want to tire you out!" He moved to the big trunk. Its hump in the middle sported two strips that wrapped all the way around the trunk. He tried the latch, but it didn't budge.

"Is it locked?" Dave wondered.

"I think so," Mr. Warren replied. "Where would we find a key? Maybe it's hanging somewhere from a nail, or maybe it's in a dresser drawer. Everyone keep on the lookout for a mysterious key."

Jodi and Cheryl opened a box. There were old-fashioned baby clothes, and nestled underneath a baby blanket was a cigar box. "Look at all these old love letters," said Cheryl. She took them to Mr. Warren. "Do you know any of these people?"

Mr. Warren thumbed through the faded envelopes. "I'm not sure who this lady Ella Smith is," he mused. "Here's a letter written in Spanish!" Then his eyes sparked with recognition. "Here's one I know. It's Chester Warren, my great-grandfather! This is a great find, Cheryl. I'll take these downstairs and research them. Larry, would you please take these down to my office and put them on my desk, and then bring back a marking pen? Thanks."

When Larry returned, Mr. Warren wrote on the box, "Chester Warren's Time." Meanwhile, Larry opened the dresser drawer. "Here's a set of rings," he called with a sound of victory. He held up a clump of keys, held together with string.

"Good job!" Mr. Warren exclaimed as Larry handed him the keys. Everyone gathered around the old trunk. The first key was too big; the second key was too little. The next key went into the keyhole, but nothing budged as Mr. Warren turned the key first one way and then another. When all the keys had been tried without success, Mr. Warren sighed with disappointment, "I was hoping this would work," he said. "So keep looking."

Larry went back to the dresser. Jodi was looking in a box with old dishes wrapped in yellowed newspaper. And Cheryl began walking slowly around the room, looking up and down the studs and rafters. It wasn't long until her voice rang out, "Here's a key!" Mr. Warren went to where she was pointing. A key hung from a nail on the back side of a stud. He smiled and carefully lifted the key from its hiding place.

Again the group gathered breathlessly around the mysterious brown trunk. Mr. Warren inserted the key, and the latch clicked open. "Yeah," the young people chorused.

"Good job, Cheryl," Dave grinned at her in admiration. "You've got a good eye!"

Mr. Warren slowly lifted the lid to the trunk. The removable shelf on top was divided into compartments. Inside were war medals, an old pistol, a small jewelry box, an old doll with a porcelain head, handkerchiefs, and a lady's fancy white hat covered in netting.

Mr. Warren carefully lifted the top shelf out of the trunk and laid it on the floor. "Oooh," the girls whispered as they saw what was lying in the trunk. It was a beautiful old wedding dress. Mr. Warren carefully lifted it out and handed it to Jodi. Cheryl helped her unfold the dress, and they admired the satin and lace, the ruffles and tucks. "I wonder who the bride was," Jodi said.

"And here's the hoop skirt and old-fashioned underwear to go with it," chuckled Mr. Warren, as he handed more garments to the delighted girls.

The boys were admiring a military uniform that lay folded in the trunk, and wondering who wore it. There were a few other items of unusual clothing next. They were made of thin material, and the top was decorated with fancy stitches up and down its length. "These look like they are from the Philippines," Mr. Warren mused. "I wonder what their story is."

Next lay a hand-crocheted tablecloth and a log-cabin quilt. On the very bottom of the trunk lay a decorated box. Mr. Warren carefully lifted it out and removed the lid. "It's a photo album," he said with joy. "And here's a diary. Perhaps these will give me a clue as to who owned all these things. I hope some of you can help me with the research." He set aside the album, the war medals, and the jewelry box for closer exam, and then carefully replaced the other items back in the trunk.

"I think we've done enough for today," Mr. Warren announced. "Let's mark the boxes we've explored, and save the rest for another time."

"Thank you for showing us all these things," Larry said as he helped the others carry Mr. Warren's treasures down the steep steps.

When they had all finished placing the things in Mr. Warren's office, they heard Mrs. Warren's pleasant voice, "Everyone, please wash your hands. I've got a treat for you in the kitchen." Warm cookies and milk greeted them as they sat down at the table to enjoy a snack.

"Thanks, Mrs. Warren," Cheryl smiled warmly. "We've all had such a good time today. But we should probably be going home now before it gets dark."

As they were all saying their good-byes. Larry slipped something into Dave's hand. "It's your turn for a while," Larry said. "Enjoy!"

Dave looked down at the object in his hand. It was the black bag with ORB inside. Larry had just given him the special glasses that connected them with their guardian angels. "Thanks, buddy," Dave said as he slipped the bag into his pocket. "I'll take good care of them."

Chapter 20

The Accident

It had been a full day. Larry, Cheryl, Dave, and Jodi had watched the angel athletes perform. The storm had passed over. They had explored the Warren's attic for family mysteries.

After the friends were gone, and the evening meal eaten, Grandpa Warren suggested they gather in the living room for a while. "Dave, I want to include you in something that our family has done for years," Grandpa began. "Every evening we read a portion of the Bible together and pray to God. We've done that since your mother was a little girl. Do you mind?" His eyes searched Dave's face for a response.

"I would love that," Dave said. "It was the Bible that led me to you, and I have so much to learn about it."

Grandpa opened the Bible. "I'm reading from the Psalms. They are a collection of ancient songs, poems, or prayers that people wrote to praise God." Grandpa's steady voice began reading:

The earth is the Lord's and everything in it,
the world, and all who live in it;
for he founded it upon the seas and established it upon the waters.
Who may ascend the hill of the Lord?
Who may stand in his holy place?
He who has clean hands and a pure heart,
who does not lift up his soul to an idol or swear by what is false.
He will receive blessing from the Lord . . .

When Grandpa had finished reading, Dave longed to tell Grandma and Grandpa about ORB. The words Grandpa had read reminded him of his trip to R-dor, when he had "ascended to the hill of the Lord." Surely his grandparents would understand about ORB, he thought. They believe in God and his kingdom. They believe in following God's holy ways. But now Grandpa was praying. His words sounded like a conversation with his best friend. It reminded him of the times he talked to D-go, his guardian angel.

When Grandpa said "Amen," Dave made his decision. Pulling ORB from his pocket, he began. "I want to show you something very special." He unzipped the black bag and opened the glowing case so the glasses could be seen.

"Amazing!" commented Grandma as she peered at the glasses.

"Larry and I found these in the woods last fall. When we put them on, we can see in the fifth dimension. We see our guardian angels working for God's kingdom, and we see the evil angels trying to destroy it."

"Interesting," Grandpa said. "May I have a look?"

"Sure," Dave handed the case to his grandpa. "Never mind the tingling sensation you get at first."

Mr. Warren put the glasses to his eyes. He saw the guardian angels keeping the dark angels from entering the room. He was amazed, and let Mrs. Warren have a turn.

"Tell us more of what you have learned," Mr. Warren probed.

"Our angels have told us so many important things," Dave began. "And they've shown us some unbelievable things, too. We (my friends and I) have decided to belong to God's kingdom. And we want to help God's team by doing what we can to help rescue the people who are wrapped up in the webs of the evil angels. There's a boy at school who is so trapped by the evil angels, he can't even act normal."

"That's too bad," Grandma sympathized. "So how can you help?"

Dave replied, "My angel told me to just keep trying to talk to him and be friendly to him. Todd is so trapped he hardly hears the voice of his good angel anymore. He has a better chance hearing a human voice."

"I see," Grandma murmured. "Perhaps you'd like to invite him over for a sleepover sometime. It might be easier for your friendship to develop with fewer people around."

"Maybe," Dave said. "But at school, he acts like none of us are around anyway. He's a loner." After a little pause, Dave had a question. "So how did you come to know about the Good One and his kingdom—did you find the Bible all on your own?" He remembered when ORB had helped his friends and him find the Oracles.

"It happened for me a long time ago," Grandpa remembered. "My family went to church each week. My parents gave me a Bible one Christmas, and bit by bit I read and learned about God and his kingdom."

"You are so lucky to have known him for so long," Dave said, "and I'm so lucky to live with you!"

"We are very lucky," Grandma smiled, giving Dave a warm hug. "This has been a wonderful conversation. I hate to change it, but you need to get your rest, young man. We don't want you to have to go back in the hospital again!"

As Dave was getting into bed, he decided to talk to D-go and get an update on the angels' battle. He put ORB to his eyes and began laughing. There was D-go lying peacefully on the bed next to his! He appeared to be asleep, but then he turned his head and opened one eye. Dave spoke first. "I'm glad you're safe from that surprise attack. I wasn't sure what would happen to you when the enemy arrived at the games this afternoon."

D-go yawned, "Yes, the battle was fierce for a while, but Guerdon came to our rescue."

"That's good! Did you hear me talking to my grandparents tonight?" Dave wanted to know.

"Yes, I did!" D-go answered. "Good job! They are good people."

"What do you think about church?" Dave asked. "That's how Grandma and Grandpa learned about Good One's kingdom. Should I go with them?"

"Church is usually a good thing," D-go said. "But realize that the evil angels go there too, trying to make trouble, and to get some of the churchgoers on their side. There are lots of churches out there. Some are big. Some are small. Some keep the spirit of the Good One in their lives. Others go the way of the world. Some churches worship on the seventh day of the week (Saturday) because God set that day apart for humans in the beginning and blessed it. Others worship on the first day (Sunday) to celebrate the day of the week Guerdon came back to life after they killed him."

"Guerdon got killed? You mean on his secret mission?" Dave was amazed. "How could that have happened?"

"It is very amazing, and it was part of the Good One's plan all along," D-go replied. "When Guerdon (or Jesus) came to earth as a human, Hesperus hoped to cause his secret mission to fail. You see, Jesus's mission was a rescue plan for humans. It had two goals. One was to show humans what life would look like to live in harmony with God's kingdom all the time. The second goal was to make it possible for humans to live in harmony with God. He wants them to live with him forever in his kingdom where there was only love . . . no hate, no evil."

"That sounds good to me," Dave commented.

De-go continued, "The problem is that earthlings have failed to live in harmony with God's kingdom. They fall prey to Hesperus and his schemes. And Hesperus, who loves to accuse everyone except himself, has told God that humans are not good enough to live with him in 'His Very Good Kingdom,' and because they're bad, they should die forever."

"Hesperus is sure mean!" Dave exclaimed.

"For sure!" De-go agreed. "So when Jesus came to earth on his mission, Hesperus tried to discourage him from completing his mission. That didn't work, so he tried to scare him off. Finally he persuaded the human church leaders and the crowds to force the governor to kill Jesus. They tortured him to death by hanging him on a cross. It was awful to watch him die." D-go shuddered as he remembered the scenes.

"The strange thing about it," he continued, "is that now God has an answer to Hesperus's accusation that humans are bad and should die forever. God has answered by saying that he will forgive the bad things they've done and heal them by taking away the webs the evil angels have spun. That way, humans will be in harmony with God's kingdom. And if Hesperus insists that anyone should die, Guerdon has already done that for them. Hesperus's plan became a victory for God. And the wonderful thing is that Jesus came back to life again after three days. Among churchgoers, that day is celebrated on Easter."

"Wow," Dave murmured. "The story gets more and more wonderful."

"It is," said D-go, and then with a playful grin, he added, "And I have talked your ear off! It's time you go to sleep now so I can get some rest!" He shut his eyes and snuggled into the bed next to Dave's.

* * *

The Christmas vacation passed all too quickly. With the Warrens' tender care, Dave recovered quickly from his hospital stay, and was settling in nicely in his new home with his grandparents.

When the first school day after vacation came, it was nice to hear Grandma's cheerful voice waking him up. So much had changed in Dave's life since his last school day. After a warm breakfast and a pat on the back, he headed for school. His new home was so close to school that he could walk there. He would miss riding the bus with Larry, but maybe he could get to school about the same time as his bus and surprise him.

As Dave waited for Larry's bus, another bus stopped at the curb. Some senior high school students got off the bus first and waited around the bus door as if expecting someone else. One by one other young people got off the bus. Then Dave saw Todd coming down the steps of the bus. Just as his foot was about to connect with the sidewalk, Josh, one of the big boys, slid forward and pushed his foot against Todd's, knocking him off balance. Todd toppled to the pavement face-first. His backpack landed with a thud beside him. His enemies laughed and disappeared.

The bus driver was stepping from the bus to investigate when Dave rushed to Todd's side. "Todd, Todd, are you all right?" Dave asked. Todd did not stir. Blood oozed from his nose onto the sidewalk.

"Someone, call the school nurse, quick!" the bus driver called urgently.

"Todd, wake up," coaxed Dave in alarm. Students began gathering around the accident scene and whispering something about the boy being dead.

Just then the nurse and a teacher hurried up. The nurse carefully turned Todd over and checked to make sure he was breathing and felt for a pulse. "What's his name?" she questioned.

"His name is Todd," the bus driver and Dave replied at the same time.

"He should regain consciousness soon unless there is a bad concussion," the nurse murmured almost to herself. She wiped the blood from Todd's nose. "Todd, Todd, wake up," she pled. Turning to the teacher, she said, "I think you'd better call an ambulance. He's not coming to."

As the teacher disappeared into the school to phone, the nurse turned back to her patient. Larry's bus pulled up, and its students stepped off the bus. As they passed by the accident scene, several recognized Todd lying there. They were not interested in him and continued on into the school. The other students also began leaving the accident scene. Larry joined Dave, and they continued to stand nearby. "Did you see what happened?" the nurse asked.

"Yes, I did," Dave answered. "The kids were getting off the bus, and one of the big boys came back and tripped Todd as he was getting off the bus. He fell just as you found him."

"You'll be filling out a report?" the nurse looked up at the bus driver. He nodded.

Before long the ambulance arrived and whisked Todd away. Dave was deep in thought as he went into the school. "Not so long ago, that was me lying on the sidewalk," he mused. "I hope Todd gets well as I did."

Chapter 21

Family Mysteries

When school was through for the day, Dave and Larry paused outside the door. The cool wind made them catch their breath and shiver.

"I want to find out about Todd," Dave's teeth were chattering.

"I'll go with you," Larry replied. Together they went to the school nurse's office, but the door was locked, and all was quiet within.

"Hmmm," Dave said. "I guess we'll have to go to the hospital and ask there." He pulled his cell phone from his pocket to let his grandparents know that he would be late. When Dave had finished his call, he had a pleased look on his face. "Grandpa says he'll come to the hospital and drive us home. They're still making sure I keep well."

"I'm glad they're that way," Larry responded. The boys zipped up their coats and started off at a brisk pace toward the hospital.

The gray hospital building sprawled across several blocks and was landscaped with lawns and evergreen shrubbery. The boys were becoming all too familiar with this facility. They saw the Emergency Entrance. An ambulance was parked nearby. "Shall we check there first?" Larry asked.

Dave shrugged. "I guess so." They walked through the double doors to the receptionist's window. "We're looking for our friend, Todd Jones. Is he here? The ambulance brought him in this morning from school."

The receptionist checked her list. "No, we don't have him here in the Emergency Department, but he may have been admitted to a room in the hospital." She directed the boys to the main hospital entrance.

At last, someone was able to direct Larry and Dave to a hospital room. Todd was lying in bed with his head propped up. The bed sheets were drawn up to his chin, and he looked straight ahead, staring blankly at a TV program.

Dave and Larry grinned in greeting. "You sure look better than you did this morning," Dave began the conversation lightheartedly. There was no response from Todd.

"I saw the guy who tripped you," Dave blurted out. "He sure is a mean character."

At this, Todd nodded. "I've gotten myself in a heap of trouble again." He continued staring at the TV screen.

"Why *you*?" Larry questioned. "It was the big bullies that should be in a heap of trouble."

"Dad says it's my fault for making them mad at me," Todd mumbled. "He doesn't have the money to pay the hospital bill, so he's mad at me."

"I have a dad that's always mad at me, too," Dave sympathized. "But he's in prison now, and I live with my grandparents."

Todd turned to look in Dave's eyes. "I wish my dad was in prison." Todd's voice sounded full of revenge. "It would serve him right!"

* * *

When they left the hospital, Grandpa Warren was waiting for them in the car. "How is your friend?" he asked.

"Todd's awake, and his body is doing better. I think he'll be able to go home tomorrow," said Dave. "But he's very discouraged. His father blames him for the accident and for costing him a lot of money."

Grandpa shook his head sadly. "I think I'll stop by school tomorrow and find out if there's anything the school's insurance can do about that." Then, a sparkle lit up in his eyes as he quizzed, "Guess what I've discovered today?"

"What?" Dave responded eagerly.

"I've been looking at the treasures from the attic today. I learned some interesting things!" Grandpa explained, "The stack of old love letters was written by my great-grandfather Chester while he was away fighting in the Civil War. He was writing to his sweetheart, Ella Smith, who wrote the other letters back to him. The diary was written by Ella after they were married in June 1866. They came west by covered wagon to Oregon after their marriage, and the diary tells of their trip. It's very interesting. After settling in Warrenville, they had eight children. One of them was my grandpa William."

When they got home, Grandpa led Dave to his office. The photo album was open on his desk, the letters were stacked in several piles, and the diary had yellow post-it notes sticking out to mark special pages. Mr. Warren pointed to a yellowed picture in the old photo album. A somber couple looked back at them. The groom was seated on a chair, and the bride stood beside him with her hand resting on his shoulder.

Dave squinted to read the printing underneath the picture. "Harriet Robinson and William Warren—June 8, 1902."

"Those are my grandparents," Mr. Warren said. "See the dress she is wearing, and the uniform he's wearing. They are the ones in the trunk upstairs. He fought in the Spanish American War."

Mr. Warren scratched his head and picked up an envelope. "This is the letter I don't understand where it fits into the picture. It comes from the Philippines, and is written in Spanish. Perhaps Grandpa made friends with someone during the war, and they kept in contact. I just don't know . . ."

"There's a person at Mr. Foster's work that can translate Spanish into English," Dave offered. "Remember the bottle we found on the beach when we went camping? It was also written in Spanish, and he got it translated for us."

"What a good idea!" Mr. Warren said. "I'll see that Mr. Foster gets this. I'll be happy to pay if there's a fee for the services."

* * *

After the evening meal, Dave went to his room upstairs to read his e-mails and use ORB. He had mail from Larry:

> *I got an e-mail from Angelina in the Philippines. She is now writing in English. She was happy to know about the Bible. She is the youngest of five children, and goes to school in Manila. She*

says she has family in the United States, but she has never met them, since they came here so long ago.

See you tomorrow.

When Dave had turned off his computer, he opened ORB's case. "Greetings, my *kanana,*" D-go grinned.

"I want to rewind to see the hospital scene with Todd," Dave explained. He was glad to see how Todd's good angel was helping Dave and Larry with just the right words for Todd. He was able to hear them.

"Keep up the good work," D-go encouraged. "I also have some words of wisdom for you and Larry. Don't forget about Jodi. She is being lured away by an angel from the legion of false love."

"Thanks for the tip," Dave said. "I'll tell Larry."

* * *

The next morning, a few minutes before the school bell rang, Dave saw Jodi talking to a guy from the senior class. His heart sank when he recognized who it was. It was the student who had tripped Todd.

"Larry . . . Larry," Dave called to his friend, who was just disappearing into homeroom.

Larry turned around. "What's the matter?" he asked.

"Come here! Jodi may be in trouble soon if we don't do something," said Dave with a serious expression. "Look who she's with!" They stood outside the homeroom door, watching Jodi as she smiled and responded to the young man's attentions. He walked very close to her, his hand on her shoulder. As they reached the homeroom door Larry and Dave overheard the student say, "I'll see you after school."

"Oh, hi," Jodi greeted Larry and Dave as she almost bumped into them. "I haven't seen you for a while."

"I know," Larry felt awkward. "We've been busy because of Todd's accident. We went to visit him in the hospital yesterday."

"Who was the guy you were talking with?" Dave asked.

"Oh, it's Josh. He's a senior, and he's been really nice to me," Jodi responded with a self-conscious smile.

"I'm glad he's nice to you. He wasn't so nice to Todd," Dave remembered yesterday's accident.

"Really," Jodi said, "he has very nice manners."

"Jodi," Dave urged, "I wish you'd come to my place after school and use ORB. You'll see how Josh acted then."

"I wish I could," Jodi apologized. "But Josh promised to give me a ride in his car after school today. But I probably could tomorrow."

Just then the bell rang, and the three scurried to their desks.

Chapter 22

Going Together

Larry had a hard time concentrating on his classwork for the rest of the day. He kept thinking about Jodi. She was so nice and cute and such a good friend. She had such pretty eyes and winning smile. He had even shared the secret of ORB with her. He thought that someday, their friendship would blossom into something special. Now there was Josh in the picture. How could he ever compete with Josh, a senior? He had a car. Larry didn't even have his learner's permit yet. All he could offer Jodi was a ride on his bike. Not much competition there, he thought.

When the last bell rang, Larry and Dave walked slowly into the hall. If they dawdled enough, maybe they would get another glimpse of Jodi with Josh. Perhaps an opportunity would come that would help the situation. They made their way toward Jodi's locker.

"I have ORB with me," Dave said, changing their focus. "If it works out for you, I thought I'd stop by your place, and we can talk to our angels. And," his face blushing a bit, "I thought Cheryl might like more time with ORB."

"That's a good idea," Larry agreed. "There's nothing we can do with Jodi when she's with Josh, so we might as well hurry and catch the bus. It will save a few steps." Their pace quickened.

As they jumped aboard, they looked for an empty seat. "There's Cheryl," Dave's voice sounded a bit eager. "Let's sit behind her." As they slid into the seat, Larry noticed Jodi getting into Josh's red car. He groaned inwardly. What could he do? It would be good to talk to L-mor about the problem.

Cheryl turned around in her seat. "So Dave, how do you like your new home?"

"It's great!" Dave replied with a smile. "Which reminds me, I need to call Grandma or Grandpa and tell them where I'm going. Excuse me for a second."

In just a few minutes, they had reached their bus stop. They chatted as they made their way to the house. "I brought ORB," Dave told Cheryl. "I thought you might like to spend some time talking to your angel. They can really help answer your questions."

"I would love that," Cheryl said. "I've been so amazed at what I've learned so far."

"Larry needs some time with ORB too," Dave confided. "I found out last night that the evil angels are plotting to trap Jodi. Today, we saw her with Josh, and she seems to think he's pretty nice. But D-go says that he is being used to lure Jodi away from the Good One's kingdom. We all need to come up with a game plan."

As they started up the walk to Larry and Cheryl's house, Tiger jumped off the front steps and trotted to meet them. Larry stooped to pet Tiger's head, and Tiger stood on his hind feet so his head would connect with Larry's outstretched hand. "Are you glad to see me, old boy?" asked Larry. Tiger rumbled and rubbed on Larry's legs. It was hard to get inside the house without tripping on Tiger.

While Larry spent some time with ORB talking to L-mor, Dave, and Cheryl chatted. Dave had always thought of Cheryl as a sister. After all, she was his best friend's sister, and Larry was almost like a brother. But now that he lived with his grandparents and had few problems at home to worry him, he began to think about his friends. What would it be like to have a special girlfriend? Cheryl was certainly attractive, and she was available. She shared their interest in ORB and the Good One's kingdom. He wondered what she thought of him. Right now, her eyes were focused on him intently as she listened to him talking. It made him feel important. He enjoyed talking to Cheryl.

Dave told her about Todd's accident and how Josh was responsible for it. He told her about Grandpa's discoveries with the pictures and albums they had found in the attic.

"There was just one envelope that Grandpa couldn't figure out," Dave remembered. "He was going to talk to your dad and see if someone from his work can translate it for him."

"I'm sure Dad will be happy to do that," Cheryl said.

Cheryl's turn with ORB took a long time. With her keen mind, she had so many questions she wanted answered. "So how long will the war between good and evil last? When will it end?" she asked C-tel.

"I can't say exactly," C-tel replied. "Only the Good One knows. Sometimes he compares the war to a farmer growing crops. When the fruits and grains or weeds are ripe, he will come to harvest the good crops and destroy the weeds. As time goes by, the struggle between good and evil will get more and more intense. Hesperus will almost destroy the earth in his attempt to capture earthlings for himself."

C-tel's face brightened with a happy smile. "But when the Good One is satisfied that everyone has had a chance to choose between his kingdom or the evil kingdom, he will send Guerdon to earth to collect his faithful followers. It is recorded in the Bible in chapter 24 of Matthew. Guerdon's coming will be a glorious event, and we angels will all come with him to collect our *kananas.* After his children are safe, he will put an end to Hesperus and the evil angels, and the war will be over. There will be a huge celebration party when that day comes." C-tel clasped her hands together and pulled them to her heart.

"I really want to be in God's kingdom," Cheryl said earnestly to C-tel. "I believe all you've told me. Please rescue me from these webs wrapped around me and keep the evil angels from trapping me again!"

"We surely will," C-tel happily flicked away the webs and then hugged Cheryl. "Just remember that when you see terrible things taking place, it means the fighting is getting fiercer. Even though it will be a hard time for everyone, it will help people make their decisions one way or the other. In the end, God will win!" C-tel smiled with confidence.

While Cheryl was taking her turn with ORB, Larry shared with Dave some of the conversation he'd had with his angel. "L-mor says that the evil angels are using Josh to lure Jodi away. You already knew that, but I had to hear it for myself. He says we should still try to be with Jodi as much as she'll let us. We can tag along, letting her know that we're still friends. Any of her friends—even Josh—are our friends too, you know. (That will be a stretch for us!) We are to watch out for the crisis so we can be there when it comes to her."

Dave nodded and gave Larry a knowing look. "Like Grandpa was there when I had my crisis," he said thoughtfully. "It sounds like we're to be Jodi's human guardian angels!"

Larry laughed, "I think you're right. L-mor also told us to read a Bible verse where Jesus gives us advice about enemies."

"That's cool," said Dave. "What is it?"

"Luke, chapter 6, verse 27," replied Larry. He opened his Bible, found the verse, and began reading:

> *But I tell you who hear me: Love your enemies, do good to those who hate you.*

"Hmm," Dave pondered. "That's going to be hard to do."

"I know," Larry muttered. "I feel like spray-painting a hate message on Josh's fancy red car! But L-mor said we don't have to love our enemies on our own power. Good One and Zephyr will give us the strength. Here's another verse that follows shortly." Larry read:

> *Do to others as you would have them do to you.*

"I've heard that before," said Dave. "I think Grandpa calls it the 'Golden Rule.'" Larry and Dave repeated the words over again. There was a nice sound to them. It would be a good thing to remember when dealing with people like Josh or Winnie.

Then Dave had an idea. "I'm going to ask my grandparents if you *all* can come over tomorrow evening, even Jodi, so she will have a chance to use ORB. Maybe she'll listen to J-gette's warnings. And maybe she'll be able to see what Josh is really like. We can all see the picture of my great-great-grandparents wearing the wedding dress and uniform, and see if we can get Grandpa to help us find that secret passage."

Just then, they heard Mr. Foster's voice. "Dad's home," Larry commented.

"He's probably home for supper," Dave reasoned. "I'd best be getting home."

But on the way out, Mr. Foster called, "Dave, I have your grandfather's letter translated. Would you be so kind to take it to him?"

"Sure," Dave agreed as he took the letter.

"You know, the address on this letter has a very familiar ring to it," Mr. Foster noted. "What's the address of the girl in the Philippines who sent the message in the bottle?"

"32 Blanco Road," Dave read the return address on the envelope and his eyes widened with wonderment. "I think that's the same address as Angelina's!"

Now he had to know for sure and raced back up to Larry's room. "Do you have Angelina's address—the message from the bottle?" he asked excitedly.

Larry opened the desk drawer and pulled out the creased note. Dave set the letter next to the note. "The address is the same! How can that be?"

* * *

Dave could hardly wait to tell his grandparents the strange coincidence with the letter and Angelina's address. Breathlessly, he handed the letter to Grandpa. "Read me what it says. I can't wait!" Dave bounced around Mr. Warren.

"Okay, okay. This is what the letter says":

> *Dear Mr. Warren,*
>
> *I hope you and Mrs. Warren are well. I am sorry to write this letter in Spanish. I promise to learn English as soon as we arrive in America. My wife and I thank you for your kind offer of work and the tickets for passage to San Francisco and then to Oregon. We look forward to meeting you in person and serving your family faithfully.*
>
> *Sincerely, Carlos Cortez*

"Do you know that his address is the same address as the message in the bottle we found!" Dave exclaimed. "This must be a relative of Angelina's!"

"What a coincidence! It would appear that they're related," Grandpa mused. "They apparently came to the States to work for my grandparents."

"That's cool," Dave said.

Later that evening, Dave made arrangements with his friends to come home with him after school the next day. Then he sat down to talk to his grandparents. They listened to the day's happenings of Dave and his friends. Grandpa shared about his visit to the school to inquire about insurance coverage for Todd, and then his visit to the hospital to make sure all the financial arrangements were in place.

"Todd's father will not have to pay anything," Grandpa reassured Dave. "You can tell Todd when he comes back to school."

"Thank you, Grandpa," Dave was encouraged. "That will make Todd feel better."

"I can see we have many things to talk to God about tonight," Grandpa said with a smile. Dave nodded.

* * *

Todd was at school the next morning. He was sitting at his desk, staring absently at the desktop. Dave made his way to Todd's side. "Glad to have you back. You look a bit better than the last time I saw you," Dave smiled.

Todd nodded slightly, his eyes still focused on his desktop. "My dad made me come," he said through teeth that were almost clenched, his eyes flashing angrily. "He hates me. Everyone hates me."

Dave ignored Todd's comments and continued, "Grandpa checked on your hospital bill, and your dad won't have to pay anything." Todd didn't respond, but continued to stare at his desktop. Just then, the bell rang, and students scrambled to their places.

Larry looked across the room at Jodi. She was busy reading something. It looked like an unfolded note. It was probably something from Josh.

When English class was over, Larry worked his way to Jodi's side. At least he had the advantage of being in the same classes with Jodi. "I'm looking forward to our time at Dave's house this afternoon," he said. "Mr. Warren is going to help us hunt for the secret passage."

"Sounds fun," Jodi responded, but the enthusiasm was not in her voice. Larry was worried that she was thinking that secret passages were more interesting for children rather than mature people like herself.

When school dismissed, Larry, Jodi, and Dave waited near the school door for Cheryl to join them. A red car stopped in front of them, and Josh's voice called out, "Can I take you home, Jodi?"

Jodi hesitated. Larry answered for her, "Not this afternoon. We all have plans. Maybe another time."

Jodi looked confused. Josh responded to Larry sarcastically, "Are you all going for a bike ride?"

"Nope," Larry shook his head.

"Going to play on the swings and slides?" Josh mocked.

Just then Cheryl joined them. "Who's that rude guy?" she wanted to know. Jodi looked embarrassed.

"He's just a competitor for Princess Jodi's time," Larry said as he motioned the group to move down the sidewalk away from the car. The car's tires squealed as it lunged forward and roared away.

Jodi began to laugh. "Princess Jodi! Where did you come up with that?"

Larry shrugged and grinned mischievously. "I don't know. Maybe ORB will tell us."

Mrs. Warren welcomed the young people at the front door. "And how was school today?" she wanted to know. "Come have some cookies and milk while you tell me."

Mr. Warren joined them soon, and when they were finished with their snacks, he led the way into his study. He was anxious to show the kids the pictures of his grandparents wearing the clothes they had discovered in the attic. "But the mystery gets more interesting with the letter from the Philippines. It's so remarkable that the address is the same as the message in the bottle. I hope that Larry will find out more about Angelina's relatives, to see what the connection is." He smiled at Larry.

"I'm working on that, Mr. Warren," Larry told him.

"Grandpa," Dave began. "I'd like to show you something that Larry and I noticed in the closet in my room. We wonder if it has anything to do with the secret passage you've told us about."

"Really!" Mr. Warren exclaimed, showing immediate interest. "Let's go have a look." When everyone had arrived in Dave's room, he opened the double doors to the closet.

"We noticed that the shelves on this end are made with a different wood than the ones at the other end," Dave said, pointing to the shelves. "They look newer, and we thought maybe they had been built over the opening to the secret passage."

"That's an interesting concept," said Mr. Warren, examining the shelves and tapping on the wall. "I see the closet wall does not go as far as the bedroom wall does, which would leave a space inside the wall," he said excitedly. He looked at the walls outside Dave's room. He then checked the walls and ceilings downstairs. Everyone followed, waiting for his verdict. "I see that this space enclosed for the fireplace brickwork is larger than needed. I believe we're on to something. I will call a carpenter tomorrow to remove the shelves in your closet so we can explore further. Will that be okay with you, Dave?" Mr. Warren asked.

Dave's eyes danced with excitement. "It will be fine," he said with enthusiasm. "I will make sure the shelves are empty. I really don't need them anyway."

"Okay," Mr. Warren said. "I will leave you young people now so you can have some time alone." He grinned and winked at Dave.

As he closed the door behind him, Cheryl commented, "He's sure a nice man, Dave."

"I think so too," Dave responded with a pleased smile. Pulling ORB from his pocket, he handed it to Jodi. "You didn't get a chance to talk to J-gette last night, so you go first. The rest of us can work on an e-mail to Angelina."

Jodi hesitated as she put ORB to her eyes. She wasn't sure she wanted to hear what J-gette had to say. She watched the incident that happened after school when Josh invited her to ride with him. She looked closely at Josh. He had a lot of gray webs spun around his head, his heart, and his hands. J-gette called Jodi's attention to a few strands of gray webs that were wrapped around her heart. "You can take away my webs," Jodi pleaded, "but I still want to be friends with Josh. He's cool. I'd like to help him know about Good One's kingdom. I'd be the perfect one to help him."

J-gette looked sadly at Jodi. "It doesn't usually work that way," she explained. "You are a human, and you're dealing with evil angels. They didn't get their name because of the decorations they wear. Their webs are powerful chains. I can remove your webs, but because of your attraction to Josh, the webs will come right back. We've worked with this type of thing before, and you are the one that is usually hurt. Josh will talk nicely to you, but it's because he wants something for himself."

"For himself?" Jodi questioned.

"Yes," J-gette replied. "For himself *and* Hesperus's kingdom. Be on your guard."

When Larry's turn came to use ORB, he found a little silver piece in the case with the green glasses. Larry grinned at L-mor. "What's this?"

"It's for your k-sun. You stood up to Josh in a strong yet respectful way this afternoon. It took courage to do that. It would have been much easier to call him the bad names that the evil angels were suggesting you call them."

"Really?" Larry snapped the silver piece in place.

"Why don't you rewind ORB and see for yourself?" L-mor suggested.

As Larry watched the scene through ORB's lenses, he was amazed to see the flurry of black darts flying at him from the evil angels. L-mor and D-go were dashing here and there, removing and intercepting the poisonous darts. Larry was successfully dodging some of the darts as well. When the evil angels realized they were not going to win this battle, they scowled with hatred. Angrily, they pushed Josh's car off to a speeding start, howling in tune to the squealing of the tires. They vanished from sight.

* * *

When Cheryl got home, she plopped down on her bed and opened a note that Dave had handed her. He had been paying more attention to her lately. She had caught him looking at her, and then self-consciously turning away when he had been discovered. She wondered what he had to say. Most likely, he was too shy to say something to her. She read:

Dear Cheryl,

I think you're awfully cute. I'd like to go out with you. What do you think?

Dave

Chapter 23

The Stolen ORB

Cheryl smiled as she reread Dave's note. "I thought something was happening between us," she said to herself. "He's not the type I would consider a 'hunk,' but he's thoughtful and kind. He and my brother have introduced me to ORB and the angels in Good One's kingdom. And he has a very cute smile."

The next morning, Cheryl followed her brother toward his classroom, hoping that she would find Dave. She waited outside the door for a few minutes, and was almost ready to leave for her own class when Dave came into sight.

"*Yes,*" she said coyly when he was close enough to hear. "Yes, to the question in your note." Her eyes sparkled.

Dave blushed and smiled.

"I'll be off to class now," Cheryl announced with an air of buoyancy. "See you after school!"

"All right," Dave said to himself as he almost floated into his classroom.

Todd lay with his head on his desk. Dave noticed him and walked to his side. "Todd, are you feeling okay?" he asked. There was no response. "Todd, are you awake?" Dave tried again.

A muffled voice answered, "Leave me alone."

"I was just wondering if we could eat lunch together," continued Dave.

"I don't have a lunch," the voice responded.

"I'll share some of mine with you. Grandma always packs too much for me," Dave persisted. Todd raised his head. "I'll meet you after third period, and we'll go to the lunchroom," Dave said and added, "I would like that."

Meanwhile, Larry was struggling with how to act around Jodi. This morning, she was not her usual self. She seemed absorbed in thought, and made no eye contact with Larry. "Now I understand how the Good One feels when his *kananas* ignore him," he thought. He remembered L-mor's counsel, and it gave him patience to wait for the right opportunities to show Jodi his concern and loyalty.

When it was lunchtime, Dave found Todd, and they started for the lunchroom. Todd walked as if he were unsure of himself. Dave wondered if perhaps Todd had never eaten at the lunchroom before. Some of the students bought their lunch at the cafeteria, and some brought lunches from home. Apparently, Todd had not done either enough times to feel confident with the process.

Dave led the way to a table, set his backpack down, and unzipped it. He pulled out a sandwich and handed it to Todd. Then Dave searched for the rest of his lunch, as it had shifted down into the pack. As he pulled out another sandwich, he heard a plunk on the table. It was ORB! Quickly he scooped up the black bag and put it back in the backpack. If Todd had noticed ORB, he did not let on. He seemed focused on his sandwich and oblivious to Dave. But it was hard to tell with Todd.

Dave munched on his sandwich and tried to start up a conversation, but it was not easy. "What do you do for fun when you're at home?" Dave asked.

Todd was stuffing big bites into his mouth as if he were really hungry. At last he swallowed and said, "I don't have much fun at home." He took another bite and then continued, "But I guess target practicing is the most fun I have. My dad likes to hunt. He has a gun collection and lets me practice shooting, sometimes rifles and sometimes pistols."

"I remember you telling me you lived a long ways out of town," Dave offered his friend some chips. "You can shoot guns where you live?"

"Yeah, we have no neighbors," Todd explained. "There are lots of trees around. Sometimes I get a squirrel or a bird. But most of the time, I just shoot at bottles or cans."

Dave picked up an apple. "Do you want this? I don't have any way to divide it."

Todd reached in his pocket and pulled out a pocketknife. He opened a blade deftly, cut the apple in halves, closed the knife quickly, and slipped it in his pocket. Dave pretended to ignore the knife even though it was not allowed at school. He opened a bag of cookies.

When the boys had finished eating, they walked toward the door. Dave noticed Jodi sitting with Josh at a table in the corner of the room. And then he began to chuckle. At the table next to Jodi's sat Larry and Cheryl. They must be shadowing Jodi today, acting as human guardian angels!

"I'm going to talk to my friends over here. Do you want to come along?" Dave asked. Todd followed automatically.

Dave caught Cheryl's eye, and she smiled. A warm feeling swept over him. "Todd and I were just having lunch," he explained. Just then something stung him on the face, and a peanut fell on the table.

"Oh," Todd moaned as he noticed Josh. "It's the guy on the bus I hate."

Another peanut hit Todd. They could hear snickering from the next table, and a sarcastic voice said, "Well, well. If it isn't loser boy!" More peanuts flew at them. Dave and Todd tried to dodge the flying ammunition.

"Quit it," Todd yelled. "Bully!"

At that, Josh stood up. His form towered over them. "What did I hear you say?" he questioned threateningly.

"Don't answer him," Dave cautioned Todd in a whisper. "It'll only make matters worse."

"You keep out of it *loser-lover*, eating lunch with this loser!" Josh yelled as he lunged for Dave. He grabbed Dave's backpack and yanked it away from him. He swung it over his head and taunted Dave.

"Are you going to tattle to the teacher?" Josh sneered. Larry and Cheryl stood up to join Dave. Jodi looked on helplessly, fear in her eyes.

"What would you like us to do?" Larry asked boldly.

"I'd like all you mosquitoes to disappear," Josh quipped back.

"We can do that," Larry retorted, "just as soon as you return the backpack."

"I'll return it," he said, recklessly unzipping the backpack and emptying the contents on the floor. "Here's your backpack," he smirked, throwing the empty backpack toward the group.

"Josh," Jodi pleaded. "These are my friends. Be nice to them!"

"Be nice to them?" Josh repeated with a smile. Taking Jodi's hands, he pulled her to a standing position beside him. "Then come along, Jodi. For your sake, I'll leave them alone." He scuffled through the items on the floor, kicking books and belongings here and there as he and Jodi left.

The friends helped Dave gather his things from the floor so he could put them into his backpack. It was then that they realized Todd had disappeared.

"Where's ORB?" Dave asked anxiously. "I can't find it!" They searched the area thoroughly, but ORB was nowhere to be found.

"Who took it?" Larry wondered. "I didn't see anyone pick up anything off the floor."

"It's got to be Josh," Dave said. "We've got to talk to Jodi and see if she knows anything about ORB."

It was a sad group that made their way back to afternoon classes.

Chapter 24

Crisis at School

Todd was not at school the next day or the next.

Larry tried to talk to Jodi as often as possible. With Josh in the picture, that was more and more challenging. Larry told Jodi about how ORB had disappeared after the scene in the lunchroom. But she hadn't seen ORB and didn't think Josh had taken it.

Larry, Dave, and Cheryl longed to talk to their angels, but with ORB missing, that was impossible. So when they got together, they read sections from their Bibles and talked about the meaning of it. Some things were hard to understand, so Dave talked to his grandparents to see if they knew what it meant.

The week passed slowly.

Jodi was becoming more and more comfortable with her relationship with Josh. And Jodi's mother was getting used to the idea of Jodi having a special boyfriend. So when Josh asked Jodi to go to a movie with him on Friday evening, her mother agreed.

Josh picked up Jodi just before 6:30 p.m. Even in the dusk, the shiny car was impressive. She felt so grown up as she slid into the seat beside Josh. She hoped there would be time this evening to talk to him about the Good One's kingdom and the invisible struggle that was going on with the good and evil angels.

Josh cruised up and down Main Street a couple of times, hoping there was someone to impress along with Jodi. He saw a couple other cars of guys that he knew, and they waved at each other and revved their car motors in response. But Josh spotted a police car parked inconspicuously along the main drag. So he gave up his cruising and drove to the movie theater.

As they found their seats in the darkened theater, Jodi noticed violent clips showing on the screen. Josh had not told her which movie he had chosen, and she had forgotten to ask. She hoped it would not be a movie that emphasized the evil ways of Hesperus's kingdom. But as the dark action-filled movie progressed, Jodi began to feel more and more like a traitor to Good One's kingdom. She covered her eyes with her hands when the gunfights and explosions were too scary to watch.

"What's the matter, dear?" Josh whispered with a grin. "Can't you handle all the action here?" He slipped his arm around her shoulders and squeezed her. "This is exciting! It's fun!" But somehow, his hug did not comfort her.

When the movie was over at last, Jodi was relieved. "I'd like to go home now," she said.

"Home already?" Josh questioned. "I thought we could find a nice, quiet place and talk first."

Jodi shook her head. She had a feeling of impending doom and was impressed that she should go home where it was safe.

"Ah, come on now," Josh begged. "You're a big girl. You don't have to go to bed when the little kids do."

"I'd really like to go home now," Jodi insisted.

"We will in just a bit," Josh cooed. "But first I want to show you something." He steered the car to a road leaving town. "I want to show you where I live."

Jodi was quiet. Josh seemed intent on getting his way, and was refusing to listen to her.

"You're sure quiet. You're not pouting, are you?" Josh pretended to be sympathetic.

"There doesn't seem to be much point in talking," Jodi muttered quietly, "unless someone listens."

"I'm listening," Josh laughed. "But it's the car that doesn't listen. It wants to go home!"

Just then, the car skidded and slid abruptly into a long narrow lane and stopped. Josh turned off the motor and lights, and turned toward Jodi. "That's my house way at the end," he said, nodding toward a few lights flickering in the distance. "No one will bother us here, and we can have a nice quiet talk. The moon is shining all romantic like. And you're my special girl."

Josh reached behind the seat and brought up a bottle. "I thought you might enjoy a little drink to celebrate. This is good stuff." He popped the lid off and handed it to her.

The smell was strong. It reminded her of Christmas day at Larry's place when Dave's father was there. He smelled like this, and he was an alcoholic. "No thanks," she said. "I don't drink alcohol."

"Have you ever tried it?" Josh questioned, implying that she was naive.

"No, I don't need to," Jodi responded. "I see what it does to other people." Then she saw an opportunity to bring up the subject that was swimming in her mind. "What do you think about God and his kingdom?"

"God?" Josh asked in disbelief. Seeing Jodi's nod, he grasped for words. "I . . . I . . . I've never thought much about him. It seems like God's people don't have much fun. They can't do this, and they can't do that. I'm for having fun."

"I believe in God, and I like to have fun," Jodi said. "We learned about God through some special green glasses called ORB. They were in Dave's backpack the day you emptied everything out on the cafeteria floor. Now they're missing . . . did you take them?"

"You mean these?" Josh playfully opened the glove box of his car. There was the black bag with ORB's shiny beams barely visible through the cloth.

Jodi's eyes grew wide in surprise and delight. "Yes," she said excitedly, reaching for the bag.

"No, no, no!" Josh teased, pulling her hands away and closing the glove box. "Not unless I get something in return. How about giving me a kiss?"

Jodi hesitated. She wasn't sure she wanted to kiss Josh now, but if she could get ORB back, maybe it would be worth it. "You promise to give me the glasses if I give you a kiss?"

"Yup," Josh lied. "Now come close to me, baby. I know you are one of those respectable girls. I like that in a girl." He drew her closer to him and lifted her chin until their lips met and lingered. There was the thrill of the moment, but then he wouldn't let her go.

"Please, don't," Jodi protested, trying to get free from his grasp. "I promised one kiss. Please give me the glasses."

Josh ignored her plea for ORB and smothered her words with his lips, his grip on her tightening. She hated his heavy breaths smothering her face. She hated his lack of respect for her.

"I'm not ready for this," Jodi emphasized, trying to push him away. But Josh was stronger than Jodi, and he continued to hold her close. Eventually, Jodi realized that her pleadings were of no use to Josh. It was time for desperate measures. She struggled to get one hand free and gave him a hefty slap on the side of his cheek. "Take me home *now*," she insisted, pulling herself free.

"You want to play rough?" Josh questioned angrily. "I'll play rough!" He lunged for Jodi and grabbed her.

Somehow, Jodi was able to open the car door. With an adrenalin rush she yanked and freed herself from his grasp. Jumping out of the car, she prayed, "Help me, God!" Slamming the car door shut, she began running toward the main road.

"Ouch," Josh cried in pain as the car door slammed on his hand. "That little twerp will not get away with this," he determined. He shook his hurting hand and then started the car like a mad man. He reversed the car into the main road. He shone the lights down the road, but there was no Jodi. Perhaps she was confused and had gone the other way. He turned the car around and shone the lights the other way. Still, there was no Jodi.

He stepped out of the car and yelled, "Jodi, come back. I'll take you home now." But there was silence.

The more he thought about Jodi, the angrier he became. He would just leave her to find her own way back, he decided. He stepped on the accelerator and headed for town, leaving the sound of squealing tires and the smell of burning rubber behind him.

When the quiet returned to the country road, Jodi crawled out of the culvert she was hiding in. "Thank you, God, for showing me this culvert in the dark," she said aloud. "J-gette was right. It is no use with Josh. He won't listen to anyone except himself and his evil angels. I can't trust him. Too bad I couldn't get ORB either." The moon was bright enough that she could see the road in the darkness. She began walking home.

It took about a half hour to reach the outskirts of town. Twice she had to jump into the tall grass in the ditch and lie flat when a car was coming down the road. She couldn't risk meeting Josh again out here in the country where she was practically defenseless. Once in town, she slipped into the side streets and found her way home. She hoped her mother would be in bed by now so she wouldn't ask any questions about Jodi's dirty clothes and torn top. She thought about her friends Larry, Dave, and Cheryl. They would never have treated her like Josh did. How could she have been so foolish to neglect her good friends for someone like Josh? She knew she had hurt them and her precious angel J-gette who had helped her escape tonight from Josh.

Jodi opened her Bible and read:

> *Praise the Lord, O my soul, and forget not all his benefits—*
> *who forgives all your sins and heals all your diseases,*
> *who redeems your life from the pit*
> *and crowns you with love and compassion.*

Yes, her life had been redeemed from the "pit" this evening. She closed the Bible and slid into bed. She determined to call her friends in the morning and tell them about ORB and her decision.

* * *

Todd was troubled all weekend. It was as if a dark stifling blanket covered him. He could hardly breathe. His father had beaten him again. He knew his father hated him. The kids on the bus hated him and heckled him, especially Josh. He was sure his teachers hated him, and the students hated him, well most of them anyway.

He had escaped from his father's bad temper by going outside. The forest that surrounded his house provided a safe place for Todd to be alone with his thoughts. He took his father's pistol to shoot a few cans. But even that did not erase the pain of his thoughts. Now those painful thoughts were turning to anger. He became angrier and angrier. Life wasn't fair, and it wasn't worth living anyway. He thought about taking his own life. No one would miss him anyway.

Then he thought about those people that made him the angriest—his father and Josh. He hated them with his whole being. As he aimed the pistol at the cans, he was seeing his father's drunken face, and then Josh's sneering face. It gave him satisfaction to see the can sail into the air and skid along the ground from the force of his bullet. A plan began to develop in his sick mind.

* * *

Monday morning dawned peacefully. No one suspected the horror and evil that would cloud this day forever, except for Todd.

As students and teachers prepared for a new school day, the school became alive with activity. The students who walked to school made their way inside to their lockers to hang up their jackets and collect their books. The buses arrived one by one, and more students made their way down the hallway to their lockers.

Cheryl and Jodi had found each other and were talking happily when Josh sauntered up and interrupted them. "I think I have something you would like," he sneered, reaching into his pocket.

Just then, a gunshot was heard. Josh was hit and fell to the floor. More shots were fired, and others fell to the floor. Pandemonium set in. There was screaming, students racing to escape, moans of pain and cries for help from the wounded, and one last shot as Todd took his own life. Jodi backed into her open locker and burst into tears. Before her, Todd and Cheryl lay motionless on the floor. Blood oozed from their wounds.

A soft voice whispered Jodi's name. It was Larry, crawling on his hands and knees and stopping in front of her. "Is she alive?" He touched Cheryl's wrist and felt for a pulse. There was none. Jodi knelt beside him, weeping with him for their friend and sister. "Thank God you're alive," Larry hugged her. Tears coursed down their cheeks.

Through his tears, Larry noticed something on the floor that looked vaguely familiar. It was splattered with blood, but ORB's little black bag was a welcome sight amid so much tragedy. He tenderly picked it up, wiped it off on his pants, and slipped it into his jacket pocket.

Soon the police arrived in full force and placed the school in lockdown. The officer in charge instructed no one to move until they were told to do so. The siren of the ambulance died as the vehicle stopped at the front door of the school. Medics rushed in and prepared those who were wounded to be transported to the hospital.

Sheets were placed over those who had died. The police listened to the stories of the eyewitnesses and recorded their names.

"Have you seen Dave yet this morning?" Jodi asked.

Larry shook his head. He hoped that somehow Dave had missed the nightmare that was taking place. After what seemed a thousand years, they were permitted to leave with their parents to go home. School was closed until further notice.

When the Fosters drove into their yard, Mr. and Mrs. Warren and Dave were there with open arms to greet and comfort them.

Chapter 25

The Attack

The town of Warrenville was in a state of shock for days. People could talk of nothing else, and news reporters seemed to be everywhere. A school shooting is always tragic and created questions from all over the country. How could this have happened in the quiet little town of Warrenville, Oregon? People searched for answers and sympathized with the victims' families. Four students had died, including Todd. Three students had been wounded. Todd's father was found dead at his home, and it was assumed that Todd had killed him before he left for school that fateful Monday morning.

Larry's family was especially disrupted with the unexpected death of Cheryl. Her life had had more than its share of challenges, but she was one to rise above her problems. Her keen mind and wit had kept the family stimulated and entertained. Her absence created a deep void. It was a shock to plan a memorial service for someone who had been so young and full of health and life. Everything crashed to an end so unexpectedly. Her family was numb with grief. Friends of the family brought food and volunteered to run errands and help with arrangements.

Jodi was another one who suffered terribly. Two of her friends had died before her very eyes. The mental pictures of the tragedy stuck in her mind like concrete and gave her nightmares. Counselors had been hired to help the students process their feelings and emotions, and this was helpful for Jodi.

Dave had avoided the crime scene because he had overslept that morning and was a few minutes late arriving at school. And he felt particularly bad that Todd, the boy he had tried to befriend had become a victim and perpetrator of Hesperus's evil ways. How sad that Todd would not let Good One's team rescue him. But even more devastating to him was the loss of Cheryl. She had promised to be his special friend. His dream for her died with that fateful bullet.

The return of ORB was a comfort to the three friends. They gathered in Larry's room to talk to their angels and replay the horrible scene through the eyes of the fifth dimension. They tried to make sense of the whole event, but there were few answers. Hesperus's angels had influenced Todd's thinking to the point that he acted out on his violent mood, bitterness, and desire for revenge. And Good One's angels could not force their *kanana* Todd to do something against his will. Freedom and liberty for God's children are part of the love that is the foundation for his kingdom. Good One allowed evil to take its course, letting it triumph this time. He had something more important in mind to be accomplished in the future. But that was something only he could see. The poor humans could not really understand this.

The young people could see the good angels crying at such a terrible disaster. C-tel, Cheryl's angel, was one of those crying. She hugged Jodi and Larry and Dave as each one took their turn with ORB. "It's so sad to see Hesperus's angels claim Cheryl's life," she said between sobs. "But I know that someday soon, when Guerdon returns, she will come back to life. Good One will make all things right in the end. We have to believe that. Evil will be punished, and good will be rewarded. One day, this terrible blot in our lives will seem small compared to the wonderful future that will be ours forever. He even promises to help us forget all the bad things that have happened to us. In the meantime, Zephyr, who is sometimes called 'the Comforter' will be with you in a special way."

There were a lot of comforting words spoken at Cheryl's memorial service. The Bible verses that touched Larry, Dave, and Jodi's hearts were the words from the second book of Thessalonians.

It talked about the time that Jesus would come back to earth to rescue the good people and take them to heaven.

> *For the Lord himself will come down from heaven*
> *with a loud command,*
> *with the voice of the archangel and*
> *with the trumpet call of God*
> *and the dead in Christ will rise first.*
> *After that, we who are still alive and are left*
> *will be caught up together with them in the clouds*
> *to meet the Lord in the air.*
> *And so we will be with the Lord forever.*
> *Therefore encourage each other with these words.*

The next week, Mr. and Mrs. Warren encouraged Dave to attend church with them. They thought this might help him find peace of mind. As they parked in front of the big building, Dave saw the neatly kept lawn and shrubbery. A huge cream-colored cross stood in the middle of the grassy lawn. It matched the trim on the church. Strangers were making their way inside. Dave felt small and unsure of himself.

"Come, Dave," Grandma encouraged, noticing his hesitancy. "It will be all right. The first time is always hard."

As they walked in the door, a smiling blonde-haired girl greeted them and handed them a program brochure. "That's Rachael, our pastor's daughter," Grandma explained. "She must be about your age. Let's go find a seat now." Dave followed his grandparents to a seat. Soft music was playing, and people were whispering in low tones, greeting one another. When the service began, there was singing and music, praying, and reading from the Bible. The pastor gave a talk based on the words that Jesus spoke as recorded in the Bible. It was the last verse in John 16:

> *I have told you these things so that in me you may have peace. In this world you will have trouble. But take heart! I have overcome the world.*

These words were a comfort to Dave and Mr. and Mrs. Warren.

As the days and weeks passed, people gradually resumed their lives. School reopened, and students began to think of their studies and activities again. The addition of a security officer at school was a grim reminder that something had changed. On the whole, everyone pretended that things were back to normal. But under the surface, another struggle began to take place. Hesperus continued his attack with mind games. His forces created millions of dark darts they called "mind mines." They worked day and night, aiming the darts at the most vulnerable earthworms—the ones who were suffering from tremendous losses. The mental torture plagued these people especially. Even though Good One sent extra angels to combat this attack, the *kananas* sometimes refused to be helped. The battle raged on in people's minds.

Larry was one of these. He missed his sister. Her room stayed neat and quiet. She didn't come to borrow his baseball glove or make smart remarks. As he sat slumped at his desk, dark thoughts of blaming himself surfaced. If he had known she would die, he would have been a better brother to her. If he hadn't introduced Cheryl to Jodi, she wouldn't have been in that bullet's path.

His hand went to his heart. He felt his k-sun under his shirt, and pulled it out to look at it. Was this a symbol of his courage? If he was really growing in courage, he would have stopped Todd somehow! He had failed. The k-sun seemed to mock him. He yanked it from his neck and tossed it into the bin with the baseball bats, glove, helmet, and other gear. He heard it tinkle to the bottom of the bin. Good! It could just stay buried there for all he cared. There was no way that L-mor could convince him that he was courageous. In fact, he didn't even want to talk to L-mor. So ORB had remained untouched and hidden in the secret compartment of his desk.

Then other attacks of blaming came to mind. Why didn't C-tel and Good One's forces protect Cheryl? They said they would. They had rescued her from Winnie's friends, why not from Todd's sick plan? Maybe the angels were not for real. Maybe their story of Good One was all made up. And maybe Guerdon's rescue mission is all a myth. Perhaps the story of Guerdon dying on a cross and now being alive is a fable. And Good One's kingdom of love? Ha! If he really loved us, he wouldn't have let Cheryl and the others die. It was hard to put these thoughts out of his mind, and he let himself wallow in them.

* * *

One afternoon after school, Dave came to spend time with his friend in the familiar room. Larry was at his play station, keeping his mind from wandering to his own dark thoughts.

"Want some competition?" Dave joked.

"You're no competition!" Larry grinned halfheartedly. "But I'll let you play anyway."

After a few games of close competition, Dave brought up a sensitive topic. "How are our angels doing these days?"

"Don't know. Haven't talked to them lately," Larry mumbled. "I'm not really interested in ORB anymore. Do you want to take the glasses?"

Dave was shocked and searched his friend's eyes before answering. "You're sure?"

"I'm sure," Larry responded, jerking his desk drawer open and pulling ORB's black bag from its hiding place. "I'm done with them. They let me down. You can have them."

"But," Dave didn't know what to say. "Thanks."

There was an awkward silence, and then Dave spoke. "I'm going to church with my grandparents now. It's different, but I think I like it."

"Goody for you," Larry's tone was coated with sarcasm.

"Aren't we in a sweet mood," Dave replied, raising his eyebrows at his friend.

"I know. I've been pretty bummed out lately," Larry confessed, looking at the floor.

"I guess you have reason to be. I really miss Cheryl, too," Dave lowered his eyes to the floor to keep the tears from showing. "And Jodi is missing you."

Larry looked up from the floor to make eye contact with Dave. "Yah? What makes you think that?"

"She told me so," Dave said. "She's pretty bummed out too, if you took time to notice. She's been seeing a counselor."

Larry was quiet and looked at the floor again.

Dave stood and stepped toward the door. "Well, I guess I'll go. I think I need ORB right now. I'm getting depressed. Hang in, buddy." Larry was left alone with his thoughts.

* * *

The next Monday morning, Jodi caught up with Larry on the way to homeroom. "Wait up, Larry. Where have you been? I never see you anymore."

Larry kept walking. "I've been pretty much at home."

Jodi's voice was pleading. "Can't we Rollerblade or bike or do something? I'm getting depressed and bored."

"Maybe," he answered.

"Look at your hands. What have you been doing?" Jodi asked.

Larry looked at his hands, spattered with black-stained spots. "Nothing much," he answered, searching for words. "I . . . I . . . I was painting a model car."

"Sounds cool," Jodi responded. "I'd like to see it sometime."

"It turned out bad," Larry was making excuses. "I threw it away." He was glad they had reached the classroom so he could avoid any more questions.

After the last class, Dave caught Larry and announced, "Jodi and I are going to meet at the park near her apartment to ride our wheels. Can you come?"

"I'll think about it," Larry mumbled. But he did not show up.

Dave and Jodi played tag around the paved trails of the park, hoping Larry would come, but he did not. At last, the two rested on a park bench.

"I'm really worried about Larry," Dave began. "He blames Good One and the angels for not saving Cheryl. He doesn't want anything to do with them anymore. He even gave ORB to me to keep."

"Really?" Jodi was amazed. "He's always been so strong for God. How can we help him?"

"I don't know," Dave shook his head. "I guess he just needs to sort it all out in his head."

"Do you know what I think?" Jodi offered. "I think Hesperus's angels are wrapping their webs around him. We could find out if we had ORB. Do you have it with you?"

"As a matter of fact, I do," smiled Dave as he unzipped the inside pocket of his jacket. He lifted the glowing case from its bag and handed it to Jodi.

Jodi's face beamed as she talked to J-gette. "Yes, I am doing better, thank you," Dave heard her say. "I don't have the nightmares very much anymore. The counselor is helping a lot. When I have the dark thoughts, I am now able to get rid of them most of the time."

Jodi laughed. "I might have known you were the one helping with those black darts and the web weavers! Oh! And my mother has been so good to me. She notices me now, talks to me, and gives me hugs." There was a pause. "So what's with Larry? How can we help him?" There was another long pause. "Okay, we will. We'll ignore the prickles!"

Jodi removed the green glasses and placed them back in the case. "J-gette says to treat Larry like Good One's team does—just keep on loving him and ignore the prickles! They're working on him too. He's pretty tangled up with the anger webs."

"I'm glad for their help. We can do our part," Dave nodded. "Do you have time to skate with me a couple of blocks over? I'd like to show you the church I've been going to with Grandpa and Grandma."

"Sure," Jodi stood up. "Show me the way." They rolled leisurely along. Crocuses were blooming in yards along the street, and here and there were splashes of yellow daffodils.

"We're almost there," Dave puffed, and then slowed down as he noticed a police car parked in front of the church.

"Oh, oh," Jodi gasped in horror. "It's Larry!" Larry and a policeman were standing near the large cross in the churchyard. They were looking at black graffiti that covered the bottom of the cream-colored structure. "That's why he didn't want to talk about the black spray paint on his hands this morning."

"I can't believe our 'Mr. Good Guy' would do such a thing," Dave marveled.

"Shall we keep going and pretend we didn't see anything?" Jodi asked.

"Hmm, I think he needs to know he still has some friends," Dave replied.

"You're right," Jodi agreed. "That's what J-gette meant by loving him." They waited near the police car until the officer and Larry returned to it. The officer carried a clipboard, and Larry held a copy of the form that had just been filled in.

"Hello, Officer Wright!" Dave recognized the policeman who had investigated his case when he was found unconscious on Christmas day.

"Hello, again," the officer replied. "You look better than the last time I saw you. Do you know this young man?" he nodded toward Larry.

"We sure do," Dave spoke without hesitation.

"He made a bad choice last night, and now he's going to have to pay for it," the officer explained. "The judge will decide what his fate will be."

Larry looked like he wished he could disappear into the grate at the side of the curb. "We'll all help you through this, man," Dave slapped his friend on the back. "It'll be okay." Larry nodded hesitantly, not sure he believed what Dave was saying.

"I'll be taking Larry home, now," Officer Wright announced. "You two can be on to wherever you were going." Dave and Jodi nodded and watched the police car disappear around the corner.

"I think Larry is going to need us right now," Dave said. "He's going to have to face his parents!"

"You're right," Jodi agreed. "I can go on my wheels. I'll just need to let Mom know where I am."

"I have my cell phone," Dave spoke as he turned his bike around. "We can call when we get there."

They found a sober group when they arrived at the Fosters' home. Mr. Foster's voice was too controlled as the anger struggled within him. Mrs. Foster was on the verge of tears. Larry looked like he had lost his last friend.

"Sorry to intrude," Dave began, "but we want to find out how we can help."

"We're not sure at this point," Mr. Foster hesitated. "We have to wait for the judge to decide. I'm sure we'll have to pay for the damages to the church. Actually, Larry is going to have to pay for the damages." His steady gaze rested on his son. His eyes expressed the hurt, anger, and embarrassment he was feeling. "Whatever possessed you to do such a thing, son?" He shook his head in disbelief.

Jodi thought she knew what had possessed him. The evil angels were having their way with Larry. She heard him stammering, "I . . . I . . . I don't know."

"We should probably be going now," Dave broke into the conversation, "but we just wanted to say we're sorry. Do you know when you have to see the judge?"

"Next Thursday," Mr. Foster answered.

"Thanks," Dave and Jodi chorused. "Let us know if there's anything we can do."

* * *

Next Thursday, Dave and Jodi skipped school so they could be with Larry when he saw the judge. Larry's parents were there. Also there was the pastor of the church where Larry had spray-painted the cross. The judge was a serious-faced older gentleman. He listened to the police report, questioned Larry, and talked to the church pastor. With the judge's help, they worked out an agreement that the Fosters would oversee the repainting to the church cross. In addition, Larry was assigned to one hundred hours of community service, to be completed in one year.

After the hearing, Dave and Jodi joined Larry at his house.

"I guess I'll be mowing a lot of lawns this summer," Larry sighed. "I've got to earn money to pay Dad for the paint to fix the church cross. And for my community service, I'll be mowing the church lawn."

"We'll help you paint the cross," Jodi offered.

"I'll see if Grandpa will pay me something to mow his lawn," Dave added. "That can help pay back the money you owe your dad."

Larry looked down at his shoes, "You don't have to do that. It was such a stupid thing I did."

"I know we don't have to," Jodi spoke softly, "but we want to. We're still your friends." Her eyes searched Larry's face for some reaction. His cheeks flushed, and their eyes met.

"Thanks," he swallowed the lump in his throat.

"I have a request," Dave said shyly.

"Yes," responded Larry.

"I'd like to go to Cheryl's room, to say good-bye or something," Dave hesitated. "I can't explain it."

"I would too," Jodi agreed.

Larry thought for a moment. "I guess it wouldn't hurt anything. I'll go with you."

Slowly they opened the door to Cheryl's room. It was so quiet inside, and yet everything there reminded them of their friend. The white comforter covered the bed. A plump pillow in a matching sham perched at the head. A lamp, as well as a picture of Cheryl, sat on the nightstand near the bed. The translucent curtains with dainty pastel flowers softened the room. There was a faint scent of something sweet in the air, perhaps bath powders or perfume. The white dresser stood near the window. All its drawers were neatly closed, and on top were a few lonely knickknacks, a small chest, and a music box.

Jodi picked up the music box and turned the key a few times. The high-pitched metallic tones began tinkling the song, "Love Makes the World Go Round." The three friends were drawn to each other in a group hug.

"Cheryl, we miss you," Dave spoke softly.

Larry couldn't help himself and grinned as he heard himself saying, "Cheryl, I miss your smart remarks and your put-downs!" Dave and Jodi snickered.

There was a slight pause, and then Jodi blurted out, "Cheryl, I'm so lonely without you!"

"Cheryl," Larry's voice rose with emotion. "I'm so sorry I didn't stop that toad from killing you!" He stifled some sobs, but the effort of holding it in made his body shake.

The group hug tightened as the friends comforted one another. No one spoke for a bit, and then Dave broke the silence. "I'd like to use ORB right now and see what our angels are doing."

Jodi nodded. Larry hesitated, and then said, "Okay if you want to."

Dave pulled ORB from his pocket and put the glasses to his eyes. "The room is full of Good One's angels! And what's that?" He moved to the head of the bed. "Oh, you've got to see this!"

Dave's excitement was magnetic, but Larry resisted with a guarded voice. "Go ahead, Jodi. You look! I'm not in the mood."

Jodi shrugged and gave Larry a surprised look. She put the glasses to her eyes. "There is one evil angel here," they heard her saying. "J-gette, please get him out of here! Oh, thank you. And poor Larry! Look at all those webs!" Jodi sounded on the verge of tears, and then as she moved toward the head of the bed, she murmured, "It's gorgeous! Absolutely gorgeous!"

Jodi slipped the green glasses from her eyes and held them out to Larry. "Please have a little look. You won't be sorry," she pleaded. "It's about your sister."

Larry hesitated and then slowly reached for the glasses. Jodi was so hard to resist. He put the glasses to his eyes. He felt L-mor's warm hug, and saw the tears glistening in L-mor's eyes. He hobbled cautiously toward Cheryl's pillow. A sparkling object glistened on top.

"It's Cheryl's k-sun," L-mor explained. "Look at it closely."

The little silver piece was shaped like a crown. It was composed of numerous silver pieces, but over that, it was studded with exquisite diamonds and sapphires.

"She is safe for Good One's kingdom," L-mor explained. "The k-sun is symbolic for who she will be."

Larry looked again at the small sparkling crown. "A princess?" Larry asked through his tears.

"Yes, yes!" L-mor said with excitement. "Oh, trust him. Trust his words!" he pleaded.

"Help me to trust him," Larry begged. His body began to shake as the tears of relief flowed like a tap that had been turned on. He saw the webs around him melting away. He felt his friends hugging him again. He saw all the angels in the room gathering about them, their circle in a wider group hug. He heard glorious music.

Then L-mor handed Larry his own k-sun. "I have ways of finding things," he smiled. "You thought you'd gotten rid of it! And here's the last silver piece to cover the framework for your little fort. Your battle with Hesperus was a long struggle. Be of good courage. We are with you!"

Chapter 26

Secrets Solved

The private gathering in Cheryl's room was very healing for Larry, Dave, and Jodi. The beautiful k-sun on Cheryl's pillow, which could only be seen through the lenses of ORB, etched a comforting memory in their minds. In addition to the silver piece for Larry's k-sun, Dave and Jodi got new pieces for theirs too. Each symbolized the walk along the grief passage that each of them had experienced. Even though their walks were similar, they had grown in different ways.

There was also a healing that came mysteriously as the friends helped Larry paint the large cross on the church lawn. Mr. Foster supervised their work, and the pastor inspected the finished job with satisfaction. Mrs. Warren brought a jug of lemonade and some cookies.

Larry adjusted to the weekly routine of mowing the churchyard. Bit by bit, the friends were able to spend more time together. Mr. and Mrs. Warren were a wonderful support to the Fosters and the three friends of the PI team.

One day, when Larry and Jodi were visiting at the Warrens' home, the subject of the secret passage surfaced. "With all that's happened, I bet you've forgotten all about it," Mr. Warren teased. "I'll have you know that the carpenter came yesterday and took out those shelves in Dave's closet. Are you ready to see if the passage is up there?"

"Yes!" Dave, Larry, and Jodi chorused all at once. This would be a nice change to what they had been doing. They were ready for that. Eagerly they all made their way to Dave's bedroom.

Dave opened the double closet door. All eyes began scanning the empty space where the shelves had stood. "What clues should we look for, Grandpa?" Dave asked.

"It's hard to say," Grandpa answered slowly. "This end of the closet is most likely to be the door. Let's tap the wood in various places to see if it sounds like it's hollow behind it." He took his hammer and tapped all over the wood at the end of the closet. "See how different it sounds here in the corners than it does in the middle? I think it's hollow behind here. So look for a disguised button or handle that will open it. Feel the surface of the wood and see if you feel any unusual cracks or bumps."

The kids began looking at every inch of the wood carefully. "Maybe it's like the secret compartment in my desk," suggested Larry. "You just have to push on it a certain way."

"That's true," said Mr. Warren. "Try that." Larry pushed on different corners, first one, then another. But that did not open anything.

"This is sure a funny little piece of wood. Is it for decoration or what?" Jodi observed, pointing to a piece of wood on the inside wall of the closet. It was cleverly designed to look like a piece of the wall support system, but when Mr. Warren pushed on it, they heard a click, and one side of the wooden wall moved toward them ever so slightly.

"Yeah," Dave said with excitement. "Is it going to open now?"

"Well," Mr. Warren hesitated. "It hasn't been opened for many years. Let's carefully pry here and see if the hinges still work." He picked up a crowbar and gently inserted it in the crack. He coaxed the door toward him, and pulled it open.

"Oh," gasped everyone as they gaped into the darkness behind the door.

Mr. Warren took the crowbar and scraped down some cobwebs. "Is there a flashlight handy?"

Larry found the flashlight and handed it to Mr. Warren. "Let's all take turns with the flashlight," Mr. Warren suggested. "Then we'll see if we have volunteers to explore any further."

As they looked, they saw a narrow staircase that disappeared down into the darkness. Grandpa Warren steadied himself with the door frame and tested the first step. "It still feels solid," he noted. "But anyone who tries it should test each step before he or she puts their full weight on it. There could be rotten boards, and we wouldn't want anyone to get hurt."

"What's this string for?" Jodi asked as she shone the flashlight on a string just inside the door.

"Pull it," Mr. Warren suggested. When Jodi pulled the string, they could hear a bell ring faintly in the distance.

"Oh, Grandpa, I'd like to explore down there," Dave said excitedly.

"Okay," Grandpa agreed. "But let's make a safety plan before you do."

"He shouldn't go alone," Larry offered. "I'll go with him."

"Larry will need a flashlight, too," Jodi suggested.

"And a few yards of cord rope would be good," Mr. Warren suggested, "and a broom to sweep cobwebs out of the way."

Jodi smiled at the thought of them coming out of the passage covered in cobwebs!

"Now," Mr. Warren cautioned, "I have no idea where this is going to come out, so when you get to the bottom, why don't you give a drummer's tap with the broom handle. You can tap some as you go down, and Jodi and I will try to follow your progress from inside the house."

When everything was ready, Dave led the way into the steep narrow staircase, testing each step with a thump of the broom handle. Larry followed with a circle of rope over his shoulder.

Mr. Warren and Jodi followed the sound of the thumps to the first floor. But the thumps continued. "The passage must go all the way to the basement," Mr. Warren said in astonishment as they made their way down another flight of stairs. They could hear more thumps and the muffled voices of Dave and Larry. Then everything grew quiet. There were no voices; there were no thumps. Mr. Warren's eyes got a worried look in them.

Just then they heard a mysterious click, and the storage shelves in front of them began to move. The shelves were disguising a secret door that now swung out on hinges. And behind the shelves was a doorway where Dave and Larry stood. Their clothes looked a bit dirty, and there were a few cobwebs in the hair, but they wore big grins of success.

"That was cool!" Dave brushed dust from his pants.

"And look in here," Larry invited. They shone their flashlight into the little room at the bottom of the secret stairs. A low long shelf was attached to the wall. A dusty pad covered it.

"That must have been a place for a servant to sleep," Mr. Warren commented. "And here's the bell that Jodi rang a bit ago. There were a few hooks on the wall, and a smaller shelf."

"How did you open this door?" Mr. Warren asked, looking at the way the storage shelf was designed to hide the door.

"There's something here similar to upstairs," Larry proudly pointed to a wooden piece. "I pushed it, and the door opened."

"So how would you open the door from this side?" Grandpa wondered. "Larry, push on your latch again from inside." As soon as Larry held down the latch, Grandpa discovered another wooden piece on the storage shelves that moved. "This is how they opened it from this side."

"It sure was dark in there," Dave observed with a shudder.

Grandpa shone his flashlight all around the little room. "There's a light bulb up there, and a string," he observed, pulling the string. The light bulb was burned out.

"And what is this?" Jodi stooped down and pulled a box from under the cot. It was an intricately carved wooden box. Jodi dusted it off with her hands and tried the latch. "It's locked!" She sounded disappointed.

"I wonder if any of those keys in the attic will open it?" Dave asked.

Chapter 27

ORB's New Mission

The discovery of the secret passage at Dave's house was one mystery solved, but now the discovery of a beautiful wooden box made everyone curious. Ornate carvings of flowers and patterns decorated the sides and top. Grandma brought a dust cloth and polished the box with furniture polish until it shone. "I think this box was made in the Orient somewhere," Grandma commented. "The wood is beautiful."

But the box was locked. It didn't take Dave long to retrieve the ring of keys they had found sometime ago in the attic. Carefully Dave tried one key after another, but most of them wouldn't go in the keyhole. At last there was one that fit, and when the box opened, everyone gasped. There on top lay a beautiful open clamshell with a large pearl inside.

Taking the box to the kitchen table, they began to unpack its contents carefully. "This pearl in the shell may be very valuable. Handle it with care," Grandpa instructed. "If this box belonged to the servants, I wonder why they had this expensive pearl."

"Perhaps it is something they brought with them from their country," Grandma suggested. "Maybe they were saving it to sell in a time of need. Or maybe it was a family treasure."

"So why would they leave it behind?" Jodi asked. "It doesn't make sense."

Inside the box were some letters tied in a little bundle, but they were written in Spanish. Dave looked at the address on the envelopes—32 Blanco Road, Manila, Philippines. "It's the same address again," Dave said excitedly. "It is written by someone named Marcos."

"I should e-mail Angelina again," Larry suggested, "and ask her if she knows a relative with that name. Should I have my dad take these letters to work and have them translated, or at least find out what they are writing about?"

"Yes," Mr. Warren said. "I'm thinking that my grandparents' servants must have been relatives of Angelina. I would really like to know more about them and how they came to be connected with my family." He picked up an old picture from the box. A Filipino couple posed in front of a small flowering Rhododendron bush. "I think that's the bush in front of our house," he mused. "Of course, it's a lot larger now."

Jodi found a chain with a locket attached. She opened the locket and found a picture inside of a small Asian child. "And whose child could this be?" she wondered aloud. "Perhaps it was the servant's child or perhaps a relative they left behind in their own country."

The box had a few other jewelry pieces made from small shells and silver beads. Some beautifully embroidered handkerchiefs and bookmarks lay on the bottom. When they had looked at everything, they carefully put the contents back in the box. Larry saved out the bundle of letters, and Grandpa removed the key from the key ring and locked the box. "I'll put it on my desk for now," Mr. Warren smiled. "It will be in safekeeping until you detectives get more pieces of the mystery solved."

Later that evening Larry brought the bundle of letters down to the family room, where Mr. Foster was watching TV. He sat down with his father and began telling him about the secret passage they had discovered that day at the Warrens' house. He told of the beautiful wooden box they had found. Larry handed the bundle of letters to his dad. "We found these in the box, and they are also written in Spanish. Can your person at work translate these, too? Actually, if they just read the letters and tell us what they're about, that would be okay. I hope these letters will give us some clues as to what happened to the Mr. and Mrs. Cortez who came to Oregon to work for the Warrens."

"What an interesting day you've had!" Mr. Foster exclaimed. "I never got to explore a secret passage like that when I was your age!" Looking down at the letters, he continued, "I'll see what I can arrange tomorrow with these."

* * *

When Dave got home from school the next afternoon, there was an important letter waiting for him. "I'm thinking this might be from your father," Mr. Warren said. "It comes from the prison where he is." Grandma and Grandpa Warren gathered around Dave for support as he opened the letter. He took a deep breath and started reading:

Dear Dave,

I'm writing to ask you to forgive me for the terrible ways I've treated you. I've been a terrible father and don't deserve to be your dad. I've been told that you have recovered from your injuries and are now living with your grandparents. I hope you are happy.

Here in prison, I've been going to the group meetings for Alcoholics Anonymous. The chaplain has also given me a Bible to read. I hope it will help me get my life back on track even though it will be a long time before I get out of here.

With love,
Dad

Tears came to Dave's eyes as he reread the letter. Grandma hugged Dave and murmured, "God is helping him see the right way." Dave nodded and hugged Grandma back. He hoped to talk to D-go about this tonight.

Just then, the phone rang. Mr. Warren picked up the receiver to answer.

"This is Brian Foster," a friendly voice greeted him.

"Yes, yes," Mr. Warren said. "How are you?"

"We are fine," Mr. Foster answered. "I have some very interesting news to share with you about the translation of the Spanish letters.

Are you and Mrs. Warren and Dave available to have supper together at our place tonight?"

"Yes, of course," Mr. Warren agreed happily. "What time would you like us to come?"

"Will 6:30 p.m. work for you?" Mr. Foster asked. "I think you will want to discuss the contents of the letters with all of us. We have all been so interested in this mystery."

"We'll see you at 6:30, then," Mr. Warren put the phone down with a smile.

*　*　*

The kids could tell that Mr. Foster was eager to share the news of the letters. When everyone had finally settled at the table, Mr. Foster began, "The letters here were written to Carlos and Rosa Cortez who came to work for William and Harriet Warren about 1914. Carlos took care of the grounds and gardens for the Warrens, and Rosa was Mrs. Warren's housemaid. Carlos had been a diver in the Philippines, and so that explains the jewelry with the beautiful shells and the pearl. They had hoped to save enough money to have a home of their own. With the sale of the pearl, they hoped to be able to bring their little girl, Maria, to the States to live with them. They had to leave her behind in the Philippines, so she stayed with her uncle Marcos and his wife."

"I had an e-mail from Angelina in the Philippines today," Larry interrupted, "and she says that Marcos Cortez was her great-grandfather. The house where she is living has been in their family for over a hundred years."

"That's very interesting," commented Mr. Foster. "The letters you found span about five years, and the last letter was sympathizing because both Carlos and Rosa were not well, and Marcos hoped they would get well soon."

Mr. Foster paused for a moment. "I had to go to the cemetery today to take care of some business for Cheryl's grave marker, and so on a whim, I inquired at the office if they had anyone buried there by the name of Carlos or Rosa Cortez. To my surprise, I was directed to the graves. The markers record that they died within a few days of each other in 1919. That was the year of the terrible influenza epidemic."

Everyone was amazed at all the information Mr. Foster had found out that day. They continued talking about the sad fortunes of the Cortez family, and the little girl in the Philippines who never saw her parents again.

While Mrs. Foster was serving the ice cream and cookies, Mr. Warren was deep in thought. "So Carlos and Rosa never did get to use their pearl," he said sadly, "and my family did not know it existed. It seems like I should attempt to see that it is returned to the family."

After supper the young people gathered in Larry's room to hang out. Dave shared with his friends about the letter he had received from his father. "I'm anxious to talk to D-go about it." The friends nodded in agreement.

D-go was right there, giving Dave a hug. "How do you feel about that letter?"

"I think I'm happy about it, but I'm still not sure I trust what my dad says," Dave confided.

"That's got to be very hard for you," D-go comforted him. "Strange as it seems, your dad's going to prison was part of Good One's plan. (It wasn't the first plan he had for your dad's life, but when he wandered so far from the kingdom of R-dor, God put another plan in place to get your dad's attention.) It will take time for everything to work out, but keep hope! Good One has added more angels to help him right now. He is more willing to listen to Zephyr now than he's ever been since your mother died. In the meantime, I will be with you. And your grandparents will be with you."

"Thank you," Dave whispered as he removed the green glasses and handed them to Jodi.

Jodi smiled, sat down, and drew the glasses to her eyes.

"Hello, my dear one," J-gette greeted her, and Jodi smiled. "I've heard you processing a lot of things with your counselor, but the two of us haven't had much chance to talk about your experience with Josh and the shocking end to your relationship."

"Oh, I know," murmured Jodi. "Our relationship was over before that horrid morning at school. I learned a lesson that night in Josh's car that I will never forget. You tried to warn me, but I wouldn't listen. I wanted Josh's acceptance so much, it froze my brain."

"And have you learned something about acceptance?" J-gette pressed her.

"Yes, I have," Jodi responded self-consciously. "I'm learning to accept myself."

"Good girl," J-gette patted her on the back. "You have wonderful qualities that are very desirable. I'm sure you have seen how a certain young man in this room (who we will not mention) finds you very desirable and acceptable. Perhaps someday, he'll be brave enough to tell you!" J-gette was amused with herself and began to chuckle.

Jodi looked at Larry and began giggling. "J-gette, stop it, you are so funny!"

"Anyway," J-gette smiled, "I wanted to give you something that is well earned. It's the last piece of silver for your k-sun. From time to time, you will receive gemstones to add to your k-sun. They will symbolize your progress in your passage through life. One day, your k-sun will be just as beautiful as Cheryl's." J-gette hugged Jodi again.

As Jodi snapped the silver piece in place, she exclaimed, "It's beautiful! The etching in the silver is beautiful!"

When it was Larry's turn to use ORB, L-mor had some news that made him sad and glad. "I have had a wonderful time with you and your friends because of ORB," L-mor said. "But it is time for ORB to go on a new mission. There is another *kanana* that needs to know about the Good One's kingdom. You have received the tools you need to grow closer and closer to the ways of our Good One. You have the Bible, you have each other, and you have the knowledge that we will always be at your side to help you. Remember the game event you witnessed? Do you remember the event where we put on costumes and changed forms?"

Larry nodded. "Well," L-mor continued with a smile, "if you see a cat with a heart on his tail, it will not be Tiger. Or if you see a bird with a heart on it, it will be me coming to remind you that I'm nearby."

Larry smiled. "That's good to know. So there will be a new mission for ORB. Do I know the person who's going to get it?"

"You know her name," L-mor answered, "but you will get to know her more as time goes by. Our team has decided that Angelina will be the next one to be blessed with ORB. We have been preparing the way for some time."

"You mean Angelina in the Philippines?" Larry asked. L-mor nodded. "Wow, wait till I tell these guys!" Larry said good-bye to L-mor and placed ORB back in its case.

"Guess what?" Larry broke into Jodi and Dave's conversation. "ORB is to go on a new mission. Our time with the green glasses is almost over. They're supposed to go to Angelina in the Philippines!"

The three sat in silence for a moment, thinking about how much they would miss talking to their angels, thinking about how much they had learned from their angels. One by one, they pulled their k-suns out in the open and ran their fingers over the surface. The framework for each of the little symbols was now completely covered with silver pieces. They compared the shapes. Jodi's was like a little heart. Dave's had changed from a prison to a little house. Larry's looked like a little fort. They thought about the times that each piece had been added.

"Do you think we're finished with these?" Larry asked.

"I don't think so," Jodi answered. "J-gette said that there are gemstones to come that attach on top of the silver. Remember how Cheryl's k-sun shone with precious jewels and gems on top?"

"Hers was so pretty," Dave remembered.

Then Grandpa Warren's voice called up the stairway. "Come Dave. We need to go now."

* * *

Later that evening when Dave was alone with his grandparents, he said, "There's something I'd like to tell you."

"Yes, please tell us," Mr. Warren's kind gray eyes sparkled with interest.

"Tonight," Dave related, "when we were using ORB and talking to our angels, they told us that ORB's mission with us is almost complete. The green glasses are to be passed on to someone else who needs to know about God's kingdom. They are supposed to go to Angelina next!"

"You mean our Angelina Cortez?" Mr. Warren asked in amazement. "The timing of all these things, the message in the bottle, finding the letters, the secret passage, and now the special box with the pearl is just amazing. It feels like something God would arrange."

Dave smiled. "I know it is! Larry's angel told him they've been working on this for some time."

"Well, then," Grandpa said with a chuckle, "Do you think God would mind a little help? I think we should all fly to the Philippines to see Angelina. We can deliver the box with the pearl and give her ORB at the same time."

"Oh, Grandpa," Dave said. "Do you really think we could do that?"

Chapter 28

Saying Good-bye

Dave was thrilled at his grandfather's idea that they should all take a trip to the Philippines. Mr. Warren felt that the carved box was an heirloom and should be returned to the Cortez family. And Dave and his friends needed to deliver ORB for its next mission. He thought it would be more interesting to deliver these things in person rather than having the mailman do it.

"I'll talk to the travel agency in the morning," Mr. Warren said, "to work on tickets and hotel accommodations. We can go just as soon as school is out for the summer. And you or Larry must write to Angelina and tell her of our plans to come. Please don't tell her *why*, though. We want to surprise the family."

And so, on a warm June evening, Mr. and Mrs. Warren, Dave, Larry, and Jodi boarded a jetliner bound for the Philippines. It was a long trip, and they slept most of the way, knowing it would be morning when they arrived.

"We've crossed the international dateline," Grandpa commented as they prepared for landing, "so we've lost a whole day!"

The airport was bustling with activity as the group pushed through the crowds on the way to the baggage claim area. The sounds of foreign accents, vehicle traffic and horns, and distant church bells filled the air. A taxi took them to their hotel suite.

Larry and Jodi stood together, looking out the hotel window. Below and around were buildings coated with stucco and topped with red tile roofs. Green and flowering trees added to the landscape. In the distance, they could see the harbor with ships and boats, and behind that the ocean faded into the sky.

"This is pretty cool, isn't it?" Jodi lifted her eyes toward Larry. He was looking at her. He was struck with how pretty she was. He nodded and inched closer to her.

"I can't believe we get to do this!" Larry murmured.

Just then Mrs. Warren announced, "The taxi will be here soon, so make sure you have everything you want to take to Angelina."

The taxi wound through the narrow streets and stopped in front of a two-story stucco house. The number 32 in large wooden letters were attached to the side near the front door. The house had been painted white some time ago, but the paint had faded. A green shutter hung on one hinge, and an upstairs window was cracked. But the flowerbeds that hugged the house were immaculate and full of color.

Grandpa paid the cab driver, and they made their way up the front steps. Dave knocked on the door, and a slender girl answered it. She wore a light skirt and blouse decorated with intricate needlework. Her long black hair was pulled to one side and held in place with a flower. She smiled shyly and spoke with a slight accent, "I'm Angelina. Please come in."

They introduced themselves, and then followed Angelina into the sitting room. A middle-aged woman and man stood to greet them, and offered them seats. "These are my parents," Angelina said.

The room was tidy and clean, but the furniture worn and faded. Light filtered in from the windows making things cheerful. Mr. and Mrs. Warren seated themselves on a small orange settee, and the young people found wooden chairs of all shapes and sizes to sit on. Mrs. Warren noticed a table in the corner of the room with a beautifully carved box on top. It looked so similar to the one they had, that she could not help but exclaim over it.

"What a beautiful box," she said, pointing to the table. "Does someone in your family make these?"

Mr. Cortez smiled and motioned for Angelina to speak. "My father's grandfather made this. He made many beautiful things of wood."

Mr. Warren reached for his bag and pulled out the beautiful box he had brought with him. "Perhaps the grandfather is also the one who made this box," Mr. Warren said with a smile and handed it to Mr. Cortez. "We found this in our home in Oregon, and we think it belongs to your family. It was your great-uncle and great-aunt who worked for my grandparents many years ago. Please open the box and see the letters inside."

Mr. Cortez admired the box and carefully traced his fingers over the carved design. Slowly he turned the key in the lock.

"Ah, ah, ah!" exclaimed Mrs. Cortez as she saw the contents of the box.

The Cortez family took turns admiring the old picture and reading the letters. They examined the beautiful needlework and jewelry. Tears of joy slipped from their eyes as Mr. Cortez lifted out the pearl. Emotion filled his face. He cleared his throat and tried to speak, "This is the pearl that is told about in family stories. Great-uncle nearly died trying to get this away from a giant octopus. We didn't know what happened to it after Uncle took it to the States with him." He wiped his wet cheeks with the back of his hand. "I didn't think I would live to see it."

Angelina picked up the locket. "Open it," Jodi coaxed. "We think it might be the daughter, Maria." Angelina looked at the child's face pictured inside. She gasped and showed the picture to her parents. They looked at it carefully and then began talking excitedly.

"Come with me," Angelina beckoned, holding the locket tenderly and picking up the old photo. "I want to introduce you to Aunt Maria." She led the way to the back of the house where they entered a large bedroom. A very old lady lay in the bed, her long gray hair pulled into a braid at the back. Her face was lined with wrinkles. Her cheeks were sunken as one who had no teeth. Two brown eyes opened slowly and strained to see who was entering the room. Her thin lips moved as she lisped some Spanish words.

Angelina introduced the visitors to the old woman and explained in Spanish how they came to know the Cortez family. Then she showed the picture to the old lady. "This is your father and mother," she said. Then opening the locket, she said, "This is you!" The old woman clasped the locket in her shaky fingers and held it in front of her eyes, trying to get the picture into focus. When she realized what she was seeing, she pulled the treasures to her heart with tears spilling from her eyes.

"Madre, Padre," she whispered.

Angelina explained that Aunt Maria was 106 years old. She had lived with Angelina's family as far back as anyone could remember.

Her parents had gone to the States when she was a small child, and they had never returned.

It was heartwarming for Mr. and Mrs. Warren to see how much the box and its contents meant to the Cortez family. Mr. and Mrs. Cortez thanked the Warrens over and over again. After a little pause, Mr. Warren looked at Dave and said, "I think the young people have something they would like to share with Angelina in private. Is there somewhere they could be alone?"

"Would the balcony be private enough?" Angelina asked. Larry, Dave, and Jodi nodded. Angelina led the way through a door at the end of the sitting room. The balcony had a wonderful view of the city, and was furnished with a small table, a couple of chairs, and several potted plants.

The young people gathered around Angelina. "Remember the message you sent in the bottle," Larry began. She nodded as he continued. "You asked 'Help me find God. I want to be happy.'"

"Well, we received a gift that helped us find God. It's these green glasses," Larry said, pulling ORB from his pocket. "When you look through these glasses, you can see and talk to your guardian angel. Our angels explained so much about God and his kingdom. And now it's time for someone else to have a turn using them. You are the chosen one! Try them on. Your angel will explain everything to you."

Angelina hesitated as she examined the green glasses and wondered at their soft glow. Slowly she put them to her eyes. Immediately she smiled and started talking in Spanish. Dave, Jodi, and Larry began laughing. "The angels can speak Spanish, too!"

After a few minutes, Angelina removed the glasses and gave them to Jodi. "Your angel wants to say good-bye to you."

"Thank you," Jodi said, putting the glasses to her eyes.

J-gette was there, giving her a big hug. "Remember what a precious *kanana* you are. And remember that we, that is, the Good One, his spirit Zephyr, Guerdon, and the angels, will be with you forever. Please talk to God every day—we are a team, and you will be heard and helped no matter what." J-gette opened the palm of her hand, revealing a gorgeous gem. "This pearl is for your k-sun. (We thought it was appropriate with your trip here!) You will continue to find gems throughout your life as you pass mile-markers. It will help you remember us."

Jodi's eyes misted over as she attached the pearl on her k-sun. "I love you so much," she said as she hugged J-gette good-bye.

Next, Jodi handed the glasses to Larry. L-mor hugged him good-bye. "You have grown in courage over the past year. Continue to be strong for the Good One," he said. "Here is the first gem for your k-sun. One day, it will be as beautiful as Cheryl's. Keep watching for our gifts of gems. You bring joy to our king. Please talk to God every day—it is so important to stay connected to his power and strength."

"Thanks for everything," Larry said gratefully. He gave L-mor one last hug, and then pulled his k-sun from its place on his chest and attached the blue gem to it. He was pleased with the effect.

When it was Dave's turn, it was with emotion that he put the glasses to his eyes for the last time. "Thank-you is not enough for all the good things you've brought into my life," Dave said.

"Your story brings much rejoicing in the courts of R-dor," D-go smiled as he held a shining green gem in the palm of his hand. "This is the first gem for your k-sun, your symbol of freedom. I will miss talking to you face to face, but remember that we are always with you. Continue to shine as a light in this dark world. One day soon we will all be together again. You are loved, and God loves to hear from you every day—please talk to him." D-go hugged Dave.

Slowly Dave removed the green glasses and gave them back to Angelina. The sunlight was shining on her hair; her eyes were soft and warm. How pretty she looked. "We must keep in touch through e-mails," said Dave. "We want to know what is happening with you, your family, and God's family."

"I will," said Angelina, "and thank you so much."

When they said good-bye to the Cortez family, they knew they might never see one another again. With mixed emotions, they stepped outside just as the taxi arrived. Three seagulls flew over their heads, then circled back again.

"Did you see a red heart on that seagull?" Jodi asked.

"Yes," Larry smiled and took her hand in his.

"Did you see it wink?" Dave chuckled as his eyes followed the three birds flying playfully overhead. Dave, Larry, and Jodi waved good-bye to the gulls and stepped into the taxi.

One chapter of their lives was over, but another was just beginning.

Get Published, Inc!
Thorofare, NJ 08086
15 January, 2010
BA2010015